dixi
books

Mark Tedesco

Mark Tedesco is a writer and educator residing in both California and Italy. Mark enjoys weaving stories connecting the present to the past and exploring longings expressed in relationships, events, culture, and history.

Mark has written in the genres of travel, historical fiction, memoir, self-help, and children's fiction. His titles include: *That Undeniable Longing*, *I am John I am Paul*, *Lessons and Beliefs: Learning to Love*, *The Dog on the Acropolis*, *The Words of My Father*, *Loving Hoping Believing*, and *She Seduced Me: A Love Affair with Rome*. Mark's newest Dixi Books title, *Stories from Puglia: Two Californians in Southern Italy*, transports the reader to southern Italy to explore that region known for its history, olives, hospitality, and rich culture. Puglia comes alive as two cultures, Californian and Pugliese, interact, intermingle, sometimes misunderstand but always enrich one another.

Besides writing, Mark is an educator, and he loves to engage his students in his love of history, literature, and culture. Mark likes to travel in his off time, searching for stories that make life just a little more fascinating.

STORIES FROM PUGLIA
TWO CALIFORNIANS IN SOUTHERN ITALY

Mark Tedesco

dixi
books

Dixi Books

Stories from Puglia: Two Californians in Southern Italy - Mark Tedesco
Editor: Katherine Boyle
Proofreading: Andrea Bailey
Designer: Pablo Ulyanov
Cover Designer: Karen Snave
I. Edition: March 2023

Library of Congress Cataloging-in Publication Data
Mark Tedesco
Print ISBN: 978-1-913680-64-0
E-book ISBN: 978-1-913680-75-6
1. Travel writing 2. Italian life 3. Ancient Roman history 4. Travel tips

© Dixi Books Publishing
293 Green Lanes, Palmers Green, London, England, N13 4XS

info@dixibooks.com
www.dixibooks.com

STORIES FROM PUGLIA
TWO CALIFORNIANS IN SOUTHERN ITALY

Mark Tedesco

dixi
books

The Voice of the New Age

Table of Contents

Introduction

It is evident that the God of the Jews did not know Apulia and Capitanata; otherwise, he would not have given his people Palestine as the Promised Land
-Frederick II.

Deep in southern Italy, in the heel of the boot, is a land that I neglected to visit during the years that I lived in Italy. A friendship first drew me to Puglia, a region of Italy that I knew little about other than my friends in Rome were from there. "Come visit," they would urge me; "Puglia is the California of Italy!" Having lived in Rome, the city was my comfort zone but going that far south was not. Friendship won over my hesitancy though, and one day we jumped into our rental car and took the autostrada to a part of Italy that would change our lives.

In the days, weeks, months, and years that followed, we too were able to experience that Puglia is both a land and a people, intertwined in ways that are difficult to distinguish. The olive trees and beaches, the dances and monuments, the stories, and the towers form the Pugliesi and their land.

Two Californians colliding with the culture of the extreme south of Italy can be amusing and intriguing. We came to understand that the stories surrounding each town, building, field, and person animate the stones as much as the people in Puglia. An olive tree is not only a plant, a cathedral is not just a building, and an expat is not just a foreigner.

From Bari to olive groves, Trani to the beaches, Alberobello to the towers of Salento, these and other places gradually gave up their stories as friendship and curiosity guided us in this ongoing adventure.

The stories shared here from the past and the present begin to paint a picture of a unique place that is transformative, dazzling, and always unexpected.

Chapter 1
Olives, Olives Everywhere!

The first time we drove from the Rome airport towards Puglia, we had no idea that this area would, one day, feel like home. However, we did realize that the further south we got, olive trees seemed to outnumber the people! We were two Californians in Italy, trying not to compare everything here to everything there. Some days, we could take things as they were, without comparisons. Today was not one of those days.

"Let's think of some tourist slogans!" I suggested during the long drive. "I have one!" David replied. "Variety is the spice of life, except in Puglia. Hope you like olives!" We looked out our windows as the olive groves stretched to the horizon. "Like olives? Come to Puglia! Like anything else? Don't!" We went on and on in this vein, being the ugly American stereotypes, until one of us suggested, "Why don't we call Bruno and ask him what the fuck the deal is with zillions of olive trees?" We agreed and got our friend on the speaker phone.

"The olive tree is a symbol of our history, of the intersection of cultures that make up this land. So the trees you see are not only our economic backbone, but they point to the history that we come from," he began as we sat back for a long narrated journey.

"You have to understand the meaning behind the oil," Bruno continued. "Olives have been cultivated in this area for over 3,000 years! In the Bible, kings were anointed with oil. Another biblical story relates that an olive branch was brought to Noah in the arc to signify that the rains had passed. Oil was used to illuminate the evenings, massage the muscles of ancient athletes, and rub down senators in the grand bath complexes in Rome; it was even used as a boiling weapon and dumped on the heads of invaders. Olive oil was desired and used by all classes of society before, during, and after the Roman Empire!"

"Now look around and tell me what you see," he asked as we were driving. "Olives!" we said in unison. "Yes! You know, there are 50-60 million olive trees in Puglia, but they all stem from those first few trees brought by the Greeks, perhaps 3,000 years ago. Southern Italy, remember, was full of Greek colonies and, even in the time of the Romans, Greek was the predominant language in the south. So the olive trees you are looking at now, the hundreds and thousands of plants on each side of your car, have Greek ancestors. Before Greece, olives came from Syria and the Middle East. So what you see is a hint of our history; we were a Greek territory before Rome was even an Empire! OK, I have to hang up now; I will call you back in a few minutes!" Click.

I glanced at David and said, "The story does bring it to life, don't you think? They're not just plants; they are history!" David nodded, paused, then yawned. "Yes, but if the story doesn't have some action coming up, I'm going to start snoring," he said as he leaned back and got more comfortable.

The phone rang. "Ciao! Come va? What do you see?" he asked. "Olive trees!" we said in unison. "Exactly! Where were we? Is this interesting for you?" I said "Yes," whereas David opened half an eyelid. "Earlier I told you that olive trees have been cultivated here for about 3,000 years, but there is some indication that the history goes further back than that. I just looked this up: perhaps 8-10,000 years ago, during the neolithic era, signs of olive production were found in the excavations at Torre Canne. But it was undoubtedly the Greeks and Phoenicians who spread the cultivation of olive trees in the south, and this was then taken up and encouraged by the Romans, who had a great need for the oil produced in this area.

"Now, are you both comfortable? Because I want to read you something." I glanced over at David, who looked extremely comfortable. "Yes," I responded. "There is a town in Puglia called Giug-gianello, and in that area, there is a place called the Hill of Nymphs and Children. This place is full of stories, myths, and legends. There are sacred rocks, little Stonehedge-like constructions, and altars. The stories in this area include orcs, nymphs, evil and good spirits, witches, goblins, Greek gods like Hercules, and even saints in the Christian tradition, like St. Basil and St. John the Baptist; they are all part of this landscape.

"Nicander of Colophon was a poet who lived two centuries before Christ. He journeyed to this area and wrote down some of these stories. Don't worry; it is short! I want to read an excerpt to you.

"It is said that in the country of the Messapians near the so-called 'Sacred Rocks,' there appeared one-day dancing nymphs and that the children of the Messapians abandoned their flocks to go and look. They claimed that they knew how to dance better. These words stung the nymphs, and a competition was held to determine who knew best how to dance. Not realizing they were competing with divine beings, the children danced as if they were competing with peers of human lineage. Their way of dancing was rough, typical of the shepherds; that of the nymphs, on the other hand, was of supreme beauty. The nymphs, therefore, triumphed over the children in the dance and addressed them: 'You foolish young people, you wanted to compete with the nymphs, and now that you are defeated, you will pay the penalty.' And the children were transformed into trees near the sanctuary of the nymphs.

"Now this story is interesting because, if you go to that area where this took place, the olive tree trunks are twisted and look like faces and limbs. So families don't let their children wander in that area. Even today, some locals believe that a witch lives among the olive groves, and they fear that she will curse them."

I looked over at David; he sat up and was suddenly fully awake at the stories of curses and witches.

"We can go there if you want. There is an interesting stone monolith called Old Lady's Spindle; it is in the shape of a spindle, used to spin wool. It almost looks like a giant gold mushroom. The legends identify this stone with the one lifted by Hercules in the tales of his accomplishments. The god lifted the stone without any effort, and, throwing it behind his shoulders, he let the rock balance the way it does today.

"To bring the history back to us; look out your window now. What do you see?" Bruno asked. Again, in unison, we answered, "Olives!" Bruno chuckled. "Now, look again. Look at the tree trunks, especially the older trees you are passing. Look deeply. If you look close enough, I think you too can see the twisted bodies and faces of those who challenged the nymphs…

"Now I have to go; I will call you back in half an hour to finish the story. OK?" We agreed.

David was fully awake now and commented: "Well, maybe an olive tree isn't just an olive tree. I didn't realize that there were so many stories embedded into those twisted trunks. And to think that the oil from these trees was used for food, cosmetics, and healing! Not to mention, as a boiling weapon! We should make up a song in honor of the olive tree. What do you say?"

So we began with the Christmas song "*O Christmas Tree/O Tannenbaum*," making some slight additions.

O Olive Tree, O Olive Tree

How lovely are thy branches!

O Olive Tree, O Olive Tree

You grow in huge big ranches!

Your boughs so full in summertime,

We use your oil in wintertime.

O Olive Tree, O Olive Tree

You grow in huge big ranches!

O Olive Tree, O Olive Tree

Of all the trees most lovely;

O Olive Tree, O Olive Tree

You make my water all bubbly!

Each day you bring to us to delight

With tasty flavor in every bite

O Olive Tree, O Olive Tree

Of all the trees, most lovely.

We didn't have time to create more verses before Bruno called back. "Are you ready for what happened next?" I nodded, then realized he couldn't see me. David added, "Yes!"

"So the Romans came to power," Bruno began, "and as the empire grew, they realized what a precious commodity oil was. Until the Romans, small farmers scattered all over Puglia produced the local oil, but the Romans saw the economic value of developing this area. So the Romans purchased estates and expanded the cultivated lands. More land ended up in the hands of senators or other wealthy families, who began planting olive groves for commercial purposes. Under the Romans, the area saw tremendous growth, and the origin of many of the olive trees that you find in Puglia today stems from the trees planted at this time by the Romans. So this is another historical milestone because the olive tree in Puglia came to symbolize Roman expansionism. Now the fact that the Romans built the Via Appia through Puglia and the thriving port of Brindisi indicates the value of the oil produced here. Olive oil in the ancient world was the equivalent of crude oil today; if you could produce quality oil, you could become wealthy quickly because of such high demand. I will remind you of this story when we visit Brindisi and see the area where Roman ships came and went. They exchanged many goods there, oil being the most valuable.

"So this situation continued for centuries, and Puglia became an affluent and desirable area; its dry climate was perfect for olive groves, and more and more land was cultivated. But then something happened in 476 AD. What happened? Do you know?"

The date was familiar to me since I am a social studies teacher. "The fall of Rome?" I asked. "Exactly!" Bruno responded. "Suddenly, there was no government. There was no army. There was no money being produced. Everything centralized fell apart. In many parts of Europe, you saw the rise of feudalism, in which a lord controlled an area, hired his personal army of knights, and the peasants worked his land. But here in the south, the monasteries were able to take over cultivating the olive groves, but on a much smaller scale. Most of these monasteries were of Greek origin and followed the rule of St. Basil. You will see the connection of all of these pieces of the puzzle when we visit Otranto, where you will see the floor of the cathedral designed by a monk from a monastery of St. Basil. So, just as the monasteries kept the printed word alive during the Middle Ages when many were illiterate, they also kept the cultivation and production of olive oil alive in this area. Unfortunately, many of these monasteries have disappeared, but their legacy survives, as you can see from your window. Should I ask you what you see now?" he asked, chuckling. Again, in unison: "Olives!"

"I know I've been talking too much, so we are going to zoom forward. We are in the 14th century now..." David mouthed to me: "That's forward????" Bruno continued, "From the 14th to the 17th centuries, the production of olive oil in Puglia exploded. This oil took on a commercial value that resulted in the expansion of agriculture in this area to what you see now. Did I tell you how many olive trees are growing in Puglia today? At least 50 million! Now, I know you keep saying that you see olives everywhere, but, along your drive, have you seen any stone buildings with walls around them, some looking lived in and others abandoned?"

We had seen these isolated structures. "These are called masserie. Oil was so precious that the oil presses were often underground. Some of these were built in the time of the Romans and were still being used in the 19th century! So to guard and defend the olive production and the underground presses, in the 16th century, more groups of buildings were constructed, called masserie, where the owner and his family lived, to oversee the production. Sometimes workers also lived behind those walls, and it was a way to defend their production of the precious oil. Today many of these masserie are abandoned or converted into restaurants or private living compounds. People say that more and more celebrities purchase masserie in Puglia for their vacation homes.

"This brings us to the present. As I said before, there are at least 50 million olive trees in Puglia today, producing about 40% of Italy's total olive oil production. The production is at risk because of bacteria attacking the trees. But that, my friends, is a story for another day. What do you think?"

"Yes, another day," David responded as he got comfortable in his seat again. "I hope I didn't bore you," Bruno began to say, but I interrupted him. "Not at all!" There was a pause as we all reflected. "We began this trip by seeing countless identical trees stretching to the horizon. Because of your stories, we now see Greeks, Romans, soldiers, and monks; we see boiling oil poured on enemies, amphora shipped from Brindisi, and lamps lighting houses. We see bread dripping, athletes being rubbed down, money being exchanged, and masserie being built to guard that one precious commodity that still makes this land unique. Yes, my friend, you have brought the olive groves to life. Thank you."

Chapter 2
St. Nick: The North Pole or Bari?

Nona and Theophanes were a prominent couple in Patara, a seaport town in present-day Turkey. The year was 279 CE; they were known because they ran the most successful agricultural enterprise in the area and were often praised because of their business insight and generosity. Nona sometimes showed up in the fields, bringing baked goods to their workers as they toiled in the late morning or afternoon. "What a kind woman," one worker said one day after Nona dropped off hot loaves of bread. His companion shook his head sadly. "It's such a pity they have no children."

Being childless was a cause for shame in that time and place and left the couple with a feeling of pointlessness. Theophanes never showed his feelings on this matter to his wife, but Nona often lamented her sterility. One day, Nona was particularly depressed, so Theophanes suggested they go and speak with his brother, Nicholas, the elder, who was the Bishop in that region. Nona didn't object, so they took their donkey and made the half-day journey to the bishop's house.

Nona was middle-aged now, and her hopes of bearing a child were fading as her capacity to conceive waned. "Why am I doing this? What am I seeking?" she asked herself, as she bounced up and down on the back of the donkey, led by her husband. For his part, Theophanes simply wanted his wife to be happy and, though the birth of a child would be wonderful, he had given up that hope years ago. Perhaps this visit to his brother would give Nona the peace of mind to accept the life they were destined to live.

It was early afternoon when the couple arrived, and they headed straight into the church, prompted by an unspoken understanding between them. While Theophanes prayed for acceptance and Nona for a child, Bishop Nicholas quietly entered and sat in a corner, observing. Theophanes stood, arms outstretched, eyes closed, while Nona knelt and wept. Nicholas knew of his brother's suffering and to see their pain culminate here was overwhelming. He found his own eyes welling up with tears as he prayed, "Lord, please give them the child they long for! If you grant this prayer, I will help raise the child in your sight and do everything to help the child grow in love for you and service for the poor. Please, Lord…" he trailed off. Then his tears stopped, and Nicholas felt a flood of peace as he concluded his prayer, "Thank you, Lord, for whatever will be."

He approached the couple and whispered, "God be with you." Theophanes was thrilled to see his brother, and both embraced. Nicholas then kissed Nona on both cheeks, looking into her tear-filled eyes. "Shall we pray together?" he asked. Nicholas prayed out loud. "Just as you heard the cry of your people in Israel, hear the prayer of these good people, Lord. You know their hearts; you know what they desire and need. Please let us be open to how you work in our lives and give us what our hearts desire most. Amen."

The three left the church and, before going to dine at the bishop's humble house, they decided to go for a stroll. "How are you, my brother? And my sister?" he asked. "The fields give olives, grain, and fruit, and we are doing well. We try to do well for others and hope that we do not neglect those in greater need. But Nona suffers at times, and I will let her speak with you about that," he said, concluding.

"I am sorry you suffer, my sister," Bishop Nicholas said, taking her hand. "I feel bad because I should be grateful for everything we have been given, we have more than many others. Perhaps my desire for a child is selfish, and now that I am getting beyond child-bearing age, it is becoming ridiculous. But I seem to be unable to free myself of this longing." They continued walking in silence as the bishop seemed to be reflecting. He nodded as if he heard an interior voice. "You may bear a child," he began, "for, remember Abraham and Sarah. Everything is possible with God. And it is also possible that He plans that you remain childless. We cannot see the future and often cannot distinguish the workings of His will. However, I will make a pact with you. For nine days, we will pray that He either grants you your wish or gives you the peace of mind to accept His will. After this, you will be free and know that His plan has been made manifest. Would you make this pact with me?" The couple agreed and embraced their friend Bishop Nicholas.

After a few days, Theophanes and Nona returned to their lands but kept the pact. Life soon returned to its routines for both the couple and Bishop Nicholas as the days and weeks passed; they tended to their business and the bishop to his people. Nicholas hoped that his brother and Nona found the peace he wished for them.

In the middle of a winter night, January, in the year 280, Bishop Nicholas was woken from a deep sleep. He thought he was dreaming at first, so he lay still and heard the knocking again. It became more persistent. "Someone must be ill!" he thought, alarmed. He jumped out of his bed, slipped on his clerical robe, and looked out the window. He could not make out the figure other than a man who was knocking and knocking. He went downstairs and opened the front door. There stood his brother Theophanes, covered with sweat, panting from running, unable to speak. "What is it, my brother?" Nicholas asked, perplexed and concerned. "Is Nona alright?" At this, Theophanes threw himself into Nicholas' arms and burst into tears. "What has happened? Shall we go to her?" Through his sobs, Theophanes choked out the words, "She is with child!"

When the time came for Nona to give birth, Theophanes insisted on giving him the name Nicholas, which means "Victory of the people." He wanted to honor his brother to whom the couple attributed the gift of the child.

The boy grew and was well educated in the Greek and Latin classics and the Scriptures and came to see his namesake, Bishop Nicholas, as a second father. The bishop also tutored the boy and often brought him as he ministered to those in his territory, especially the poor.

Months became years, and little Nicholas always remembered this as one of his happiest times.

During his fifteenth year Nicholas had been staying with his uncle; one morning a message arrived from his parents. "Do not send Nicholas home next month as planned," it read. "The plague is ravaging this area, and you both are safer there. We will remain here to manage the lands and put our lives in God's hands. We are well. Mother." Bishop Nicholas read this and shook his head.

The bishop respected the instructions until disturbing news arrived a few weeks later. One of his parents' estate workers showed up at the door. "Please do not tell them that I came here since I could lose my position!" the man implored the bishop. "Yes, yes, I promise. What is going on?" he asked, disturbed. "My lady is very ill with the plague; she and my master have locked themselves inside and will see no one. We leave food, but that is all. She is dying Your Excellency! But she is afraid that her son will also come to see her and contract the illness, so they tell us nothing. But I have heard from other workers that she will not last long and that her husband, the father of little Nicholas, is now showing signs of sickness. I am giving you this information to do what you will. Now I must return before I am missed," he said, with a slight bow. The bishop insisted on giving him some refreshment, bidding the man farewell, and then entered the church to ask for guidance before speaking with his nephew.

"There is no question that I will go," little Nicholas said to his uncle once he learned the news. "These are my parents!" When Bishop Nicholas told him of his parents' concerns, he replied, "Yes, I understand. I know my parents well, and my mother has always tried to shield me from all harm. But my path is clear: I must go to them, this very day. The consequences are secondary; I will make this journey, come what will. You, uncle, should stay here where the people need you." Bishop Nicholas remained silent as he reflected. "You reason like a man beyond your years, Nicholas. I will come with you. Yes, the people need me here so I will return in two days. In the meantime, your parents and I are family, and you are like my son. Let us do this together. Can you be ready to leave shortly?" Little Nicholas nodded.

When they arrived at the estate of Theophanes and Nona that evening, they found some turmoil: Theophanes was speaking with several of his men from his window, and the workers were insisting on coming into the house to take him and his wife to get medical attention. Theophanes kept shaking his head. When the two Nicholas' came into view, the workers expressed relief while Theophanes looked shocked. "Before you say anything, Papa, I am here of my own accord, you are my parents, and I love you, and please do not object or ask anything about me being here. I respect you and love you, but if you do not come downstairs now and open the door for me, I will break it down and come in. We will wait here," the boy said, planting himself in front of the door with his uncle next to him. Theophanes disappeared from the window, and soon the front door opened. "Please do not embrace me, son, because I have the sickness also." Ignoring these words, little Nicholas put his arm around his father. "No," his father protested, weeping. "Father, some things are more important than sickness and death. Now, where is mother?" he asked. Theophanes glanced up; the boy lunged up the stairs and came into his mother's room; she was covered with bubonic swellings and moaning slightly. With her eyes closed, she seemed unaware that another was in the room.

"Mamma," the boy said. "No, Nicholas, no!" she said. "Mamma, I am here now. I know you fear me contracting the sickness, but please do not fret about this. We are all in God's hands. Uncle is here too. He will pray with you while I go to find the doctor." The boy then left his mother in Bishop Nicholas' hands.

Nona survived until the following day, when she passed away peacefully with Bishop Nicholas, Theophanes, and little Nicholas present. Before burial arrangements could be made, Theophanes became more ill and took to his bed. He called Bishop Nicholas to him and implored him to take his son as his own, see to the completion of his education, and safeguard him from all harm. "Yes, he is already like my son. But what about the management of your estate?" Theophanes looked into the bishop's eyes. "The boy must live the life that he is destined for. Neither you nor I believe his future is to be a land manager. I have put a good man in charge; he can be trusted to take over the work. In the meantime, Nicholas can stay with you and complete his education. When he comes of age, he can decide what he wants to do. Can you promise me that you will make sure that all this comes about?" Bishop Nicholas put his hand on his brother's heart. "I promise," he said.

Little Nicholas found himself an orphan a few days later. In accord with his uncle, he arranged to have his parents' bodies brought to the bishop's church and buried in the cemetery nearby. Due to the pandemic, the funeral rites were celebrated in an empty church, attended only by uncle and nephew.

Since they lived in a Greek-speaking region, Bishop Nicholas had to send for a scholar to educate the boy in Greek and Latin classics. He kept his promise and made sure little Nicholas received the best education that his resources could buy while watching over the boy's emotional well-being. "You spend a lot of time with your studies, which is good, son. And you spend a lot of time in the church, which is also good. You spend little time out of doors or with others. Is this good?" he asked Nicholas one day. The boy looked down, silent. The bishop continued, "Could it be that something troubles you, son?" Little Nicholas nodded. "There is so much pain and suffering out there. I am safe here with you. I want to become just like you, uncle, and stay here always." Bishop Nicholas smiled. "You do not want to become just like me. You must become just like yourself! I believe that if one is called to the life that I am living, one must not run away from pain and problems. Yes, son, when we love others, there is always pain. And when we get involved with the lives of others, there are always challenges. But it is by facing these things that we become what God intends." The boy thought, then asked, "So what must I do, uncle?" Rather than giving him advice, Bishop Nicholas responded, "Come with me."

An hour later, the two were standing on top of the hill, where they could see the town of Patara and the sea lapping its shores. Bishop Nicholas opened his arms. "See how glorious, son? I come up here when I begin to think that I am so important. I come here to be with the Creator. I come here when my heart needs to become simple again. You can come here with me, as long as we don't talk!

Or come on your own, or find your place in creation that speaks to your heart. We all need these places; otherwise, we begin to think that what we feel or do or fear is more important than it is."

After this conversation, the two descended into the town of Patara, where, on the outskirts, the poorer families lived. The two came upon a hut inhabited by a family of six. "Bishop Nicholas, you honor us!" the father of the house, Basil, said. The Bishop opened his arms and embraced both father and mother. "Come in, come in!" the man insisted. The hut had one window facing the sea, two chairs, and straw on the dirt floor for sleeping. "Please, please," the man insisted, giving the visitors the chairs. The man looked at his wife. "Do we have something to serve our guests?" he said to his wife's worried face. She did not respond, but Bishop Nicholas interrupted. "Please, no, I have brought food for you," and from his large pockets on his robe, he took out bread, cheese, and figs. The children came in when they heard there was food; soon, all were seated in a circle, some on the floor, two on the chairs, sharing the meal, chatting about their day, and even singing several songs. When little Nicholas looked around at the faces of the children, it almost seemed like a holiday, like a celebration of the birth of the Savior.

"I want to offer you the most beautiful thing that we have," Basil said to both Nicholas'. He then motioned them to the square hole in the wall that served as the window. The two approached and gazed out at the rolling hills before them and the harbor in the distance. "This is God's, but he shares it with us every day," Basil continued. The bishop turned and replied, "We have come to visit you, and we leave with beauty and joy in our hearts. Thank you, my friend."

Amid hugs and kisses, the two departed. "This is what charity is, Nicholas," the bishop remarked later. "It isn't just doing something for the poor; it is friendship with the poor, for in them we see God."

When the two had returned home and little Nicholas prepared their meal, Bishop Nicholas said, "You see how I live my life. Besides your studies and your prayer in the church, you also can live this life to see if it suits you. Do not be afraid of what life may bring, son, but embrace it! If we embrace life, it will, yes, bring us sorrows but also great joys. The sorrows teach us empathy; the joys teach us gratitude. We need both."

By the time he reached the age of twenty, little Nicholas was little no longer, and he was eager to mark out his path for life. "Are you certain that this is the life for you?" his uncle asked him. "Yes, uncle; I want to follow in your footsteps. I want to be a presbyter. Will you not let me take this step?" Bishop Nicholas rubbed his beard and reflected; the two were sitting in the back of the church as his nephew looked at him eagerly. "It is not a step but a journey, son. You know I would never oppose you taking this or any other course. But discerning the divine will is a process, not a moment. Be open to his will, wherever it carries you; that way, you will have no regrets. Yes, you can begin this journey." "But when?" Nicholas insisted. His uncle replied, "Now, today, this very moment. And you will begin by doing all the things you have been doing: visiting the poor, giving hope to the despairing, and asking that God use us to impart just a little bit of peace and consolation to those we meet. Besides this, we will increase some of your studies. As far as prayer, I see that you already pray much. Focus on making your prayer more simple during this time. The more simple our prayer is, the more clearly He hears us. Can you do these things?" The younger Nicholas nodded. Bishop Nicholas laughed. "I know your next question! How long, how long, uncle?" Both laughed. "We will do this for one year, and then we will see what God is asking of us. Do you agree, son?" Nicholas reached over and hugged the bishop. "With all my heart, uncle," he replied.

One year stretched into two as Nicholas passed from verification to certainty in his calling. When his uncle finally ordained him a presbyter, it felt more like a continuation than a break with the past. He ministered to the sick and poor, but he experienced a greater sense of responsibility. "Uncle," the boy-now-presbyter asked, "I still have my parent's inheritance, and yet the poor are everywhere. I am their brother and, somehow, it doesn't seem right that I have and they are wanting. What should I do?" Bishop Nicholas stroked his gray beard as he thought; after a pause, he said, "Pray, then you will find out." The boy nodded. "And I have something to discuss with you, son. I want to make a pilgrimage to the Holy Land before I am too old to make the journey. I want to leave the church in Patara in your hands until I return. The people love you; you are a man of God, and, though young, you have the wisdom to take this on. But I do not require you to do this; I ask you. Will you take care of this flock so that I can go?" Nicholas felt his eyes well up, for his uncle, in his entire life, had never asked him to do anything for him. He embraced his uncle, broke into tears, and said, "Of course, I will, uncle!"

A few months after his uncle left, Nicholas' prayers were answered, and he received the guidance that he had been seeking.

The residents of Patara were primarily farmers, able to exist as long as the weather favored the crops. There was a farmer with three daughters and no sons; his wife had died in the plague, and the daughters were approaching marriage age. The laws surrounding matrimony were strict in that culture, and a couple could not marry without the bride bringing a dowry.

"Patéras Nikólaos!" the man pleaded. "If my daughter passes the age of marriage, I do not know what we will do. She is a good girl, she has a man who would marry her, but his family will have no such thing without the dowry. Can you speak with them to see if they will make this an exception? I have no money, Patéras." Nicholas closed his eyes for a moment, appearing to pray. "God will provide," he said. The man thanked him and left.

Upon waking the following day, the eldest daughter found a small bag by the window. Someone tossed it inside during the night. "Papa, what is this?" she asked. The man shrugged as she handed him the bag. Opening it up, he found ten gold coins. "Papa, the dowry!" she cried as she embraced her father. The man was speechless as he held the coins, staring at them. "Nicholas said that God would provide." He handed the coins to his daughter and set off to thank Nicholas.

"I never said that I delivered those coins," Nicholas said, as the man insisted on showing him gratitude. "God has provided; thank Him for you and me." The man took Nicholas' hand and went to kiss it, but Nicholas pulled it back. "We can thank Him together; do you agree to thank Him and not me?" he asked. The man reluctantly agreed.

Over the following months, other acts of anonymous kindness took place. Unbeknownst to the townspeople, Nicholas had sold his parents' lands and used the proceeds to lessen the burden on his flock. Though Nicholas never acknowledged that he was responsible, the locals understood.

The word got around, and Nicholas' resources were almost depleted by the time his uncle returned the following year. "Why have you given so much away, son?" the bishop asked after a few days. "Because you said to pray, and then I would find out. Well, I did." Bishop Nicholas smiled and patted his nephew on the shoulder. "Let us go visit our people," the bishop said, "and I have something to speak with you about along the way."

That afternoon, the two spoke of many things but especially of Bishop Nicholas' journey. "Now that I have returned, son, I strongly believe that you must go. Now, don't object; I already see it in your eyes. Son, I am getting older, and I may reach the point at which I need you here. But not yet. While I was in the Holy Land, I kept thinking that Nicholas should see this, that you should experience that. These thoughts kept coming to me for the entire time I was there; I began to think that it was God who, perhaps, was calling you there. So I don't want you to respond now. I just ask you to pray and ask for guidance. Will you do that, son?" Nicholas agreed.

Somehow his uncle had planted a seed, and over the next weeks and months, it germinated from curiosity to longing and then from planning to departure. "I will not be long, uncle. If you need me to return sooner, you have my contacts." The bishop smiled. "Stay as long as you are meant to stay, and do not return early on my account, son." The two embraced, and Nicholas, having spent his whole life in Patras, embarked on a ship for the Holy Land.

Even during Nicholas' lifetime, the stories began to circulate about how, on his voyage to the Holy Land on a ship battered by a storm, the sailors begged him to ask God to save them. When the seas suddenly calmed, the sailors proclaimed Nicholas their special guardian. They reluctantly bid him farewell as he continued his voyage to the sacred lands making his way to Jerusalem to visit the legendary site where Jesus died and rose from the dead.

Over the following weeks, Nicholas traveled to Bethlehem, then Nazareth, to Capernaum and the Sea of Galilee and the Jordan River, and then back to Jerusalem. He didn't expect to feel what he did: a complete peace, a certainty in his vocation, and an overflowing love. After several months Nicholas realized that he couldn't keep his uncle waiting, so he wrote him a letter to ask for his advice. "I believe I have found my home," he said, "but I am concerned about leaving you alone. I am torn between the two. I want to stay here, but I should return to you. Help me to decide the correct path."

When he received a reply sometime later, his uncle wrote one word, "Pray." Nicholas laughed; he should have known, for his uncle had always given him the same advice. "Alright, uncle, I will pray," he said as if Bishop Nicholas was standing beside him.

It was a warm night in Jerusalem, and he tossed and turned but finally dropped off into a deep sleep when it was almost morning. His rest was filled with images and voices. When he awoke, Nicholas sat up; the repeating voice in his vision now came into his consciousness: "Return to your land, for there your path will be revealed." He lifted his eyes and asked, "Is this what you want, Lord?" Again the phrase filled his mind, "Return to your land, for there your path will be revealed."

The following day, Nicholas packed his things and boarded a ship.

His journey towards his home at Patras was almost over when Nicholas, entering the region of Lycia, stopped to rest for a few days. He was concerned about his aging uncle and sometimes wondered if he had done wrong in leaving him, but then he remembered Bishop Nicholas' words that he must find his path.

It was evening when Nicholas arrived in the city of Myra. The sun was setting over the beautiful Greco-Roman architecture as he made his way down the main street. He had run out of money, giving most of it away, and had no idea where he would stay that night. As was his custom when he arrived in a new town, he first sought out the church to give thanks for his safe arrival.

It was a simple structure in the eastern style; Nicholas entered. The interior was dark, illuminated with a few oil lamps. As he walked towards the altar, a man came towards him on his right, startling him. Nicholas froze, then noted that the man was dressed in bishop's garb, like his uncle. "What is your name?" the man asked urgently. Nicholas remained silent, looking in the eyes of the bishop, trying to discern his intentions. "What is your name?" the stranger asked again. Baffled, Nicholas asked in return, "Why do you want to know my name? I've come here to pray." Turning to go around the man, Nicholas was stopped by the stranger. "Because you may be the one," he said cryptically, motioning Nicholas to sit.

"We have been without a bishop here in Myra for some time, and my brethren cannot decide who to choose. Days go by, and we are unable to make a choice. I must return to my city, but not before a bishop is chosen for this place. My brother bishops have been meeting for weeks now, and we're about to return home without a choice when, two nights ago, one of our numbers had a dream. In this dream, it was revealed to him that someone, on a certain date and with a certain name, would enter this church, where you and I are sitting now. He understood that this was the man the Lord chose to be our bishop. So today is that chosen day, and you walked into this church before the day has come to an end. For this reason, I asked your name."

Nicholas sat there and reflected for a few moments. He looked up at the altar and prayed, "Thank you for accompanying me on my journey and please guide me home now." He got up to leave without revealing his name. He wanted no part of this, but the bishop insisted. "Please, I beg you, tell me your name!" Nicholas sighed, looked up, then looked in the eyes of the stranger. "My name is Nicholas." At this, the bishop smiled.

The two men stood in silence, contemplating the meaning of this encounter. "I must write to my uncle," Nicholas finally said. However, before he finished the phrase, he knew his uncle's response. "Pray." The mysterious bishop remained silent, then said, "I will leave you to God," and exited the church.

Nicholas turned towards the altar and asked, "What must I do, Lord?" He paused, remembering his dream. He received his answer. But still, he remained, gazing at the altar, as he thought of his homeland and his life with his uncle. Tears welled up in his eyes and fell down his cheeks. He choked on the words of sorrow and said, "May your will be done, Lord." After a few more minutes he turned and left.

The bishop was waiting outside for Nicholas. Coming down the steps, Nicholas said, "If my uncle is assisted and cared for..." The bishop interrupted him and said, "Yes, I will send a presbyter tomorrow, who will assist him and his ministry in every way!"

The bishop then saw that Nicholas had wept, he had tears still on his cheeks. He felt compassion for the man and said, "We suffer when our will is not the same as His, but I can promise you that you will once more find that joy that comes from the One who loves us more than we love ourselves." With this, the bishop embraced Nicholas and whispered, "Thank you, my brother."

With this encounter in Myra, the trajectory of Nicholas' life changed forever. Having received his uncle's blessing and the reassurance that he would be cared for, little Nicholas accepted his destiny.

After a few weeks, the mysterious man and the other bishops from that place consecrated Bishop Nicholas, who continued to serve the poor, becoming poor himself. His life ended up being one of adventure as he sought to contain the Arian heresy, which denied the divinity of Christ. He even attended the church council of Nicea in 325 CE. Under the sponsorship of Emperor Constantine, the basic tenets of Christianity were defined and expressed in what is today known as the Nicene Creed.

The people of Patras missed him, and those in Myra loved Nicholas; his big-heartedness and generosity became legendary in his lifetime. When he died in 343 CE at the age of 73, his people in Myra built a beautiful church over his tomb and named it St. Nicholas. There the body of St. Nicholas rested for over 700 years.

Several historical waves converged in Lycia as the area came under Saracen rule, thus destabilizing the Christain communities in the region. At the same time, Bari and Venice in Italy were competing to become great economic, cultural, and religious centers. Representatives of both cities were in Myra, negotiating with the Christain leadership about protecting the remains of St. Nicholas, buried under the church bearing his name. "Venice is already a great city and has the means to construct a great church honoring the saint. It will become a place of pilgrimage for the entire world," its representatives argued. "The Greek culture of Bari is a more fitting place for his remains since Nicholas also spoke the language of the Greeks," they affirmed. Months passed, but no accord could be reached.

It was early in the morning on a day in 1087 CE that the pastor of the church that bore the name of St. Nicholas came to unlock it, but he found the door ajar. Stepping inside, he looked around to see if anything had been stolen. On the right side, everything was in place, the same on the left side of the church. He then walked up the central aisle towards the altar; he saw something strange, something out of place. Suddenly he gasped and said out loud, "The bones of St. Nicholas are gone!"

Church authorities were alerted, and the Saracens were immediately blamed. "They have taken away our saint!" the local bishop cried out on the steps of the church. "We must approach the oppressors to bring back Nicholas!" another man called out. A crowd gathered in front of the church as word about what happened spread. The head of the Venetian delegation pushed his way through, entered the church, and approached the altar, peering down into a pit below the altar which once held Nicholas' bones. He shook his head, then looked around. Something wasn't right. He went to the front of the church, into the crowd, and looked around. "Where are the Baresi?" he shouted. He, and the other Venetians, went through the crowd and saw no representatives from Bari. At the inn where they were staying, the proprietor said they had left during the night. The group made its way to the port and found that their ship had departed. It dawned on the Venetians that they had been outsmarted. The bones of St. Nicholas were now on a boat heading to Bari. They had lost.

On May 9, 1087, the ship docked in Bari. Word had been sent ahead that the remains of St. Nicholas were on board, so the whole town stood waiting and cheered when the ship had come into sight and docked at the port. The anticipation grew as the crew performed their duties while several sailors were sent to bring up the saint's remains, resting in an ornate box that the captain had acquired on the voyage home.

The church leader of Bari, Archbishop Ursone, followed by a group of thirty clerics, processed down to the dock to receive the remains of the saint. Another procession met them, however: the ship's captain, sixty sailors, and the box containing St. Nicholas. "Thank you for bringing our beloved Nicholas to his new city," the Archbishop began. But he was interrupted by the captain, who asked, "Where will you lay the body to rest?" The prelate looked shocked, being unused to being addressed so brusquely. He paused, then responded, "In a chapel within the Cathedral, of course." The captain shook his head. "We will only hand over the remains of St. Nicholas if you build him a great church, in his honor, for all the people." Ursone looked the man up and down and looked at his ragtag band of sailors. "We do not have the funds for such an undertaking, but we will give Nicholas a dignified resting place," he responded. At this, the captain turned around. He signaled his sailors, and they all returned to their ship with the body of Nicholas.

The captain stood his ground, and after a few days, he and his supporters among the townspeople persuaded the Archbishop to begin constructing a grand basilica. The construction of the crypt section of the basilica started on July 8, 1087, and lasted for two years. In 1089 Pope Urban II placed the relics under the altar of the crypt, where they still lie today.

It was 1197 when the basilica in Bari was finally consecrated.

After the schism of 1054 (which resulted in the Catholic church in the West and the Orthodox church in the East), the basilica quickly became a symbol of unity between East and West. Today, in the church's crypt, there is an Orthodox and Catholic chapel for the comfort and use of Christians from both traditions. The Dominican Friars who serve at the basilica see their mission as ecumenism since St. Nicholas is honored as everyone's saint.

Pope Francis invited religious leaders from all Middle East denominations to meet in Bari in 2018. The purpose was to pray for peace in the Middle East, particularly Syria.

The tradition of St. Nicholas as the one who brings peoples together, rather than separating them, continues to this day from the tomb of that saint whose remains now lie in Bari, Puglia, Italy.

Nicholas was known for being a caring man, generous to a fault, who never sought to draw attention to himself. His faith in his God was not separate from his love for others. His message lives on.

Chapter 3
Expats: Why Puglia?

Stories of expats are fascinating because these people represent a segment of humanity that is not satisfied with dreaming. They are doers. They dare to risk everything for a way of life that they once imagined, then planned for, and now realized. This attitude makes expats among the most courageous. In Puglia, the expat community is thriving, international, and rooted in the land. Their stories give a glimpse into a way of life open to those who dare.

What is your name?

All: "My name is Sue." "Hello, I am Hanna". "We are Fergus and Ann." "Last but not least, I am Liesbet."

What is your country of origin?

All: Sue: "London, England." **Hanna:** "Austria." **Fergus and Ann:** "Australia." **Liesbet:** "Belgium."

Where do you live in Puglia?

Sue: "We have lived in Fastano, Cisterino and now in Monopoli, Puglia."

Hanna: "Martina Franca in Puglia."

Fergus and Ann: "We are living near Martina Franca."

Liesbet: "I live in Francavilla Fontana, Puglia."

How long have you lived here?

Sue: "I have lived here since 2002; I can hardly believe it!"

Hanna: "2006 is the year that I took the leap and moved to Puglia."

Fergus and Ann: "We came here to do a six-week house sit. We fell in love with the area and, once lockdown restrictions eased, we started looking at houses. We made an offer and agreed on a price; we moved to Puglia in October of 2020."

Liesbet: "Since 2013, I have lived in this great place!"

What drew you here?

Sue: "We have always been great fans of Italy, traveling here for work and pleasure over the years. Many reasons led us to Puglia. Originally we were drawn to the heel of the boot because I worked on a movie with the Italian director and actor Roberto Benigni. Once the movie wrapped, we explored Puglia, and we became mesmerized by the lure of adventure and its undiscovered secrets (a million miles from London)."

Hanna: "Our choice to move here was due to practical reasons."

Fergus and Ann: "We were drawn by the work/life balance here, where you work to live, not live to work. We found the focus on social connection and personal interaction very appealing. Added to this the great climate, the range of seasons, the hot summers, the sea and beaches, the lovely towns and villages, and the chance to learn a new language. We realized that we wanted to become part of life here.

"We have some good friends among the expat community, but our focus is getting to know the local Italians and fully integrating into Puglian life. We see ourselves as immigrants, not as expats. This place is now our home."

Liesbet: "For me, what drew me was the climate, the sun, and the language."

Why did you move here?

Sue: "It's so hard to explain why we feel so passionate about Southern Italy; maybe it is the fact that Puglia feels like the rest of Italy did 50 years ago, which is beautiful in some respects but also annoying in others. Puglia is a place where you can escape the stress of life; its seductive wildness, clear blue sea, and unspoiled coastline. We love to go to the beaches in the summer. We were desperate for this life after leaving behind the gray, miserable skies of London and being overworked- my husband's mundane job as site manager for a huge London company was very stressful."

Hanna: "My husband Riccardo (from Martina Franca originally) and I lived in Milan just before moving here. Our kids were both younger than two at the time. Riccardo had been thinking about quitting his job in banking for a while. When we learned that his father was very ill, we decided to move to Martina Franca to support his parents and prevent his family's business from collapsing. At the time, we didn't plan for this move to be permanent."

Fergus and Ann: "We left Australia in June 2019 intending to settle in Europe, probably Italy, but we were keeping an open mind. We house-sat in Czech, Portugal, Italy, and France before coming here in February. We eventually decided that Puglia is where we would put down roots.

"We love the open approach of the people, the relaxed way of life, and the focus on connection and relationships. The low cost of the basics of life also adds to the appeal here, as does the local food, wine, and other staples. We have 1.2 hectares of land and over 100 fruit and olive trees; eventually, we plan to develop the property along permaculture lines and regenerate the soil. We plan to be self-sufficient, grow our fruits and vegetables, and have minimal energy impact on the environment. In addition, we hope to get to know our neighbors and hear their stories and histories."

Liesbet: "We moved here for health reasons. We always wanted to move as pensioners, but my mum died at age 58 after two terrible years of fighting. My husband always wanted to move sooner, but I didn't until I lost my mum. I asked my husband if he still wanted to move since I no longer wanted to wait until we were pensioners. Then my health got worse; I was not allowed to get pregnant due to all my medications. I needed to be medication-free for at least six months before pregnancy. With all this in front of us, my husband said yes. We informed the family (which didn't go too well), sold the house, and quit our jobs."

Tell me about your life here?

Sue: "I still work as a make-up artist, and my work on movie sets enables me to travel the world, but I want to base more of my work in Italy. We currently live in Cisternino and, when I am not away, I enjoy my time with our little girl; I also paint and exhibit my artwork. We have also set up a small company with local Italian friends and artisans for my husband to work as a builder; we buy and sell Trulli houses. When we complete renovating a home, we usually live in it for a while, to experience life there, before selling it. We like to experience all the different towns, so we buy and sell as much as the Puglian market will allow. We choose villages around Alberobello since we can rent out properties to tourists. We found that we need our fingers in many pies to live here and survive since it is one of the poorest regions in Italy, even though tourism does well."

Hanna: "I keep very busy managing our vacation rental business, which takes up around half of my time. I enjoy looking after my kids, who are teenagers now. Besides these things, I'm involved in a dog rescue project with a local association."

Liesbet: "Our time here has had its ups and downs for sure. We live in a vacation area, but we're not on holiday as most people think. We've had a rough time the first three years. My husband was away (to Belgium) for work as my part-time job couldn't support us."

What is the best thing about living here?

Sue: "We are enjoying one of the best lifestyles and quality of life that there is. The foundation of our local society is family and community. It's undeniable that our Italian friends put a lot of importance on family, and we're very privileged to be included. Friends are never slow to break into song or dance when the mood strikes them. Italians have few equals for sheer vitality and passion for life, and life is never plain or boring. It's enthralling, intriguing, wonderful, annoying, frustrating, and somewhat backward. However, one does have to take the rough with the smooth and beautiful sunny days, delicious food, hilarious fun evenings with friends, and stunning countryside. It can't all be ups, there's an equal amount of downs too, and it's not a lifestyle for the faint-hearted."

Hanna: "The best thing for me is being self-employed, which gives me the possibility to manage my own time and to spend time with my children, as well as to explore other and new interests. I feel that this is a huge privilege. I so much prefer this life to my corporate career before moving here."

Liesbet: "The best thing for me is that I got pregnant 3.5 years after we moved, and in 2017 our Stella was born. It meant we didn't do all this for nothing."

What is the most challenging thing?

Sue: "Bureaucracy is the biggest problem; it's a never-ending hurdle, from bill paying, to local commune issues, to tax-paying and governmental decisions. Another challenge is being British and a woman in a mainly all-Italian country. Our British upbringing is incredibly different from the local people here. The men still think the women should stay at home and cook, which sounds ridiculous to a businesswoman such as myself.

"Although the quietness that comes with being behind most of the world is ideal in some ways, it is incredibly frustrating when it comes to modernization and technology.

"Italians are a volatile, aggressive, hyperactive, crazy race. Since I am British, I should be more subdued and polite (which we are known for), but you find yourself rising to the challenge and having to stick up for yourself. Admittedly here I find myself arguing and shouting like the best of them! The Italians I know are not a race to back down in an argument, and being gentle and polite has never been in their culture. If you are delicate and gentle, this is not the country to live in.

"I travel around the world for work and have spent a considerable amount of time living in other regions of Italy; I have concluded that Puglians are more hot-blooded and passionate than the rest. In Rome and Milan, the people tend to mind their own business, do not get in your face, and do not insist that they are always right and know everything, whereas Puglians do!

"Another challenge is watching our child go through the Italian education system. Schools are very backward in their teaching methods. Teachers shout at the kids, who are forced to sit for 6 hours without moving, hardly allowed to use the bathroom or drink water, no playtime, no outside time, very strict and aggressive, and this, even with the parents present!"

Hanna: "I find the local culture, here in Martina Franca, quite close-minded and conservative, reluctant to change and hesitant to embrace anything different. I realize that Martina Franca is particular due to its history and size. It is the second-largest town (after Taranto); after the war, the town created a certain level of economic growth and wealth. This relative prosperity fills the people here with pride and a certain feeling of superiority which I haven't found to this extent in other places."

Liesbet: "When I arrived, people seemed friendly but saw me as the rich foreigner or the foreigner that comes and steals their jobs. Finding work is hard, especially as a foreigner. It takes years to find the right friends and acquaintances. But you can find work as long as you're willing to work."

Do you have any regrets about moving here?

Sue: "After expressing all the challenges, I have to say that we would never leave; we love it. Yes, sometimes we talk about going back to either Ireland or England, but with all the madness, we wouldn't trade it for the world."

Hanna: "I have a few regrets. I miss being in a city (by which I mean an actual city, not something like Bari, which only has the chaos, but none of the advantages of a metropolis) with its diversity, cultural offerings, and constant change.

"I don't think the educational system is good quality. Many teachers are unmotivated; the equipment is poor, the teaching methods are entirely outdated.

"I believe the healthcare system is appalling, which is incredibly annoying since we pay the same amount of taxes for it as they do in Northern Italy, where the service is so much better.

"I'm frustrated by the public administration, which is paralyzed by bureaucracy and, to a certain extent, corruption."

Fergus and Ann: "So far, we have no regrets, but the drawn-out process of taking possession of the house we purchased was very frustrating. We miss our children and grandchildren back in Australia, but the internet makes staying connected a bit easier. We look forward to when we can go and visit them."

Liesbet: "NO! Although I wouldn't recommend it to everyone. If you're a very social person with lots of friends in your homeland, it might make it more difficult to adjust here."

Do you have any funny or unusual stories about things that happened while living here?

Sue: "I have too many to tell you right now!"

Hanna: "I have so many that I have started to collect them for a possible future book project. One example: December

2006 - I had just moved here and wanted to take the kids to kindergarten every day. I realized that tiny little snowflakes were dancing through the air as I left the house. They were so small that you could hardly see them. I put the kids in their car seats and drove to school. The roads were wet, but no trace of ice or anything like that. I had winter tires, nevertheless (which are mandatory here during winter). While driving, I noticed that I seemed to be the only car on the road but didn't think much of it. When I walked into the building, the kindergarten's only present teacher looked at me like I had just arrived from out of space.

"How could I leave the house? It was snowing!!! I replied that this was barely snow and what was the problem? This teacher said that all schools were closed until further notice to prevent all the terrible accidents that would have happened otherwise.

"I learned later that it snows in Martina Franca (which is located 400 mt above sea level) at least 2-3 times a year. Every single time it feels like a natural disaster of a major extent has taken place. I have gotten used to it now, but at the time, it did feel like being on Candid Camera."

Fergus and Ann: "We have had no amusing stories but numerous small occurrences that have brought a smile to our faces and just reinforced that this is the right decision for us."

Liesbet: "I can tell you a few of these stories. The first story has to do with driving. We have this road with many curves nearby; it is dangerous, and practically weekly, someone dies. The locals drive as if there are no curves: they drive straight, over the dividing line, on the other side of the road. When I ask some Italians: 'Why not just follow the curves? Wouldn't it be safer in case another car comes from the other side?' They reply: 'But I can't know there's a car coming from the other side,' so I tell them yes, that's why you need to stay in your lane. They look at me like I'm stupid and give me the same reply adding, 'If I knew someone's on the other side, I would stay in my lane!' So it's hopeless. The second story has to do with driving children. In Puglia, parents let their children sit and crawl everywhere in the car. When you tell them to strap their child into the chair they say no, it's not needed; the ride is short and safe. They will be protected by God or someone else, and if it happens, then it's fate. No reason to argue with that, right? The third story has to do with language. We speak Danish with our child, and when the locals hear us speak, they insist that we're German. They do not doubt it. Even if we say Belgian and speak Danish, they don't seem willing to accept that. The fourth story has to do with my name. My name is Liesbet, but 90% of Puglians call me Elisabetta or Isabel and a few other names. Even when I spell it, they hear Isabel. Strange. The last story is not so funny but is true; it has to do with healthcare. I have been hospitalized already several times, unfortunately. You have no TV, WiFi, toilet paper, etc., but the care is excellent and free. I never complain, but Italians say it's the worst healthcare, but, in my opinion, Italy has one of the best healthcare systems."

What would you tell others who are thinking of moving here?

Sue: "Life in Puglia seems like a whirlwind, which is ridiculous as we came here for the 'La Vita Bella,' but in fact, it seems to be 'La Vita Caotica.' We seem to be victims of our success in the sense of being constantly busy and on the go. Ironically, Puglia is celebrated for its simple, relaxed life, warm personal relationships and time for others, and lack of violent crime.

"You need a lot of conviction when you change your life; moving to a different country demands 100% determination. For example, we were trying to sell our British house and buy our Italian home in the middle of a terrible housing recession, but these continual problems made us even more sure that we were doing the right thing.

"Because I traveled so much, every time I got home to England, I found cloudy skies. If you see all the other beautiful places you could live in, you are more likely to want to change your lifestyle. So the weather, at least for us Brits, was a big thing and still is. We did a future forecast in 2002 to understand what the weather would be like in the coming years. It said that Puglia had one of the lowest precipitation counts of all Europe, so hardly any rain and, generally speaking-constant sun, even in the winter. We have experienced this for over 18 years now. It has made our lifestyle completely different: instead of living inside, watching TV, going to shopping malls, and staying indoors, we now enjoy being outside on the land, working, growing our organic vegetables, eating off the land, and producing our olive oil and wine. We also enjoy eating outside, relaxing, and enjoying the sun and stunning countryside. The first thing we do in the morning is to go for a walk, take our cappuccinos, and sit and enjoy the start of the day. We've found that we even enjoy our swimming pool from April to late October, altogether different from our life in the UK."

Hanna: "I believe that this is such an individual choice that it is difficult to make any recommendations. I would suggest, however, to first live here for a reasonable amount of time, possibly a year, before making the final move."

Fergus and Ann: "We have had so many people say to us they wish they could do what we are doing. We know they can; it is just a matter of having an open mind and heart and trusting what life can offer. So our advice would be just to do it. There is nothing to lose and there are so many possibilities. Yes, there are moments when we wonder what we are doing, but there are far more moments when our hearts are full of joy. We try to appreciate every moment of each day."

Liesbet: "Learn the language before you come here. We studied Italian for years and could communicate very well, but still, you're a foreigner. If they see you trying to improve, it will make the process easier; otherwise, you'll always be a 'rich foreigner.'"

How has moving here changed you? How has it changed your life?

Sue: "My husband and I had hectic lifestyles in Britain; he was a manager with a lot of pressure and an enormous amount of stress, and I traveled so much that we never saw each other. Now we have quality of life, though not without its pitfalls. We also have colorful, funny friends who are crazy. Still, they are there for you every minute that you need them: stunning landscapes and beautiful weather, hidden towns and villages to explore, endless beaches and numerous restaurants to savor, and we enjoy it all.

"Our love of architecture is unrelenting, and we continue to renovate these most unique and unusual houses--the trulli and masserie.

"Reflecting on all of this, I realize that you have to take the rough with the smooth, the insane with the sane. We wouldn't change Puglia's eclectic, ancient and backward charms for the world."

Hanna: "The move here has changed my life in every possible way. I'm not sure how it changed me, though. I have gone through many phases during these 14 years, of course, but I believe that this has to do with my general aging process, more than the fact that I live in Southern Italy."

Fergus and Ann: "It is not so much that the move has changed us but rather that we have now aligned the way we live with what we value, and we are now living an authentic life. Everywhere can have its challenges, but our response to them will determine our experience. We don't know what the future will bring, but we don't want to live a life of regret.

"Before leaving Australia, we had run a successful business providing in-home care for older people and people with disabilities. When this ended, we decided it was time for a big change. We sold everything we owned, leaving only a few boxes with family, and headed off into the unknown. We bought a small Peugeot van, and everything we owned came with us as we traveled around Europe. We had arrived with two large suitcases and little else. We did have a couple of boxes of personal items, and my bike was delivered in November. All of this fits in the back of the van!"

Liesbet: "It changed my life completely. We have a child; I'm without medication, still not pain-free but less pain for sure. I have a social life again as I couldn't do anymore in Belgium. For the last five years, we didn't meet up with friends anymore, didn't go for walks anymore (I was facing a wheelchair soon), I went to work only thanks to all the painkillers and went to bed when I got home. Boring, actually, but now we do so many things. I can still remember the first time entering Auchan and seeing the shops without thinking of returning to the car as it was parked 500m away from the entrance, and I wasn't going to make it back otherwise. We were here for about five months, and I finally was able to stop all painkillers and other meds. We were both so happy that I started to cry."

Everyone has a story: tell me your story.

Hanna: "This is difficult since I perceive my life to be a story in the making, so I don't know how to tell it yet."

Liesbet: "My story is just that when life knocks you down, you need to find a way to keep your head up every day. We need to believe we can do better and change our situation."

Is there anything you would like to add?

Hanna: "Martina Franca is just another chapter in my life. Before moving here, I must have changed addresses at least 20 times in various countries. And I plan not to make Martina Franca my last address, nor my last town of residence. As soon as the boys have finished their school here, I will leave as well... just not sure yet, where to."

Fergus and Ann: "We don't know what tomorrow will bring, but we do know we are grateful to be fully alive and living in Puglia."

Chapter 4
Is it Truly a Trullo? Alberobello

Historical site? Tourist trap? British ghetto? Real? Fake? Amazing? Charming? Boring? Which is it, Alberobello?

Everyone who visits Alberobello seems to have a different experience. Our introduction to this region was making friends; I had never heard of Alberobello back in California before meeting them. Four of us drove from Lecce, and, arriving early afternoon, we met Paolo and Gianni on an overlook, with the cone-shaped trulli houses below. I was mesmerized by the vista.

"The story of this place is tied to its name because 'Alberobello' means 'beautiful tree.' So we know that this area had beautiful trees, and it was first inhabited by farmers who worked independently to support themselves from the land," Paulo began as we all looked out at the town. "Isn't it interesting that the town is named after the trees, but tourists come to look at the buildings and don't even notice the vegetation!" He laughed as we all gazed at the teepee-like structures. "But history is made of many stories," he continued, "with many points of view. Another explanation of the name 'Alberobello' was that it derives from a specific type of tree that grew in this area; this tree, in Latin, was called 'arbor belli', which means tree of war. The wood of this tree was used to make weapons because it was a very durable material. So the town's name could be derived from the 'tree of war,' but I prefer the 'beautiful tree' explanation, so that is the story that we will remember."

Paolo paused and looked at the five of us, sitting now on the ledge, to see if we were listening. I glanced at David, who was the barometer of interest. He nodded, then Paolo continued.

"The first recorded history of the town," he continued, "wasn't until the 1400s. At this time, the land was given to the Count of Conversano by the King of Naples. The land was a reward for the Count having served in the Crusades. This man wanted to support himself through this land, so he organized a type of feudal area in which the farmers tilled and planted his land. They could keep enough to survive, and the rest had to be handed over to the Count, which he used as income."

Paolo paused and then looked at me. "Is this boring?" he asked. I laughed and glanced at David, who winked. So he began again, motioning towards the Trulli town. "Everything in Italy has a story, and the story behind these structures, the 'trulli,' is that they were constructed without cement so that they could easily dismantle them. Since the Kingdom of Naples required that taxes be paid on every building on every piece of land in its territory, our Count of Conversano, to avoid taxes, required that structures be built of local stones in the form that you see. Since the structure is held in place by a capstone, which you will see shortly, they could easily be demolished and then put back together. When tax collectors came, trulli came down. Maybe this story is true, maybe it is a legend. But I like this explanation too, so we will keep it", he said, nodding. "Good enough for me," I replied as we set off towards the tourist area.

On the way, David asked, "But what are those symbols painted on the roofs?" Not all trulli had them; some seemed to be somewhat Christian representations, others were primitive or ancient figures, while others seemed to be signs of magic. "Not everyone agrees on their meaning," Paolo continued, "but you are right. Most of them are of a religious origin: notice the symbol of the cross, and others have a symbol of the sun, both of which refer to Christ. But then there are these ancient symbols; look at that one that looks like a circle with two sticks going up: it refers to prayer rising to God. And that other one almost looks like a tree; it unites the three worlds of heaven, earth, and hell! As far as the magical symbols, if you look over there, you see a circle and a small cross, symbolizing Mercury, and on the other side, there is a symbol of Saturn. The locals often equated magic with their beliefs in the gods which were connected to the celestial bodies" Paolo stopped as we looked across at the roofs. "You know what the fascinating thing is about these symbols?" he asked. We all looked at him and waited for his answer (Paolo could be dramatic). "This one town can host three types of symbols, which indicate three different ways of looking at life: ancient, magical, and Christian. Three different world views, yet without any strife or conflict. Maybe there is a lesson for us here," he concluded.

Slightly off the beaten path, we came upon a trullo open to the public. Entering, we met the owner, a trim older man, who graciously welcomed us and explained how the trullo functioned when his grandparents lived there. A donation box near the entrance indicated that this would be a guided tour.

"See that loft above us?" he asked, pointing towards the cone of the trullo where there was a wooden platform suspended above by beams lodged in the cone. "That is where the children slept. I can remember sleeping up there when I was tiny," he said, chuckling. "Now there," he continued, "is my grandparent's bedroom," pointing to a large bed in one area of the trullo. It looked so comfortable that, without asking, I immediately sat on the bed to test its firmness. "You can lie down if you wish!" he said, laughing. I smiled as I told him how comfortable it felt. "Now in that area is the kitchen and bathroom. As you can see, they have all the modern conveniences, but it was not always like that. And in this central area," he continued, "is the living area, where the family spent time together, especially when it was cold during the winter."

I looked around and was impressed; I expected a much more primitive place, but there was something remarkable about this home. It was compact and small, but all the elements created a cozy space that seemed to draw us together. "Do you live here in Alberobello?" I asked our guide. He shook his head. "No, I live a few villages over, with my wife. But we keep this family trullo and show it to visitors when we can"

We thanked the man, dropped some coins, and wandered off towards the shopping area, where trulli converted into trinket-filled stores abounded. "Andiamo di la'-let's go over there," our friend Gianni called out. So we climbed up a street beyond the shops and immediately found ourselves in another world. Small curvy roads that snaked around the cone houses led us away from the crowds and into a more residential section. The area wasn't extensive, but it was calm and peaceful. We found a place to sit; our group of six faced each other. "What do you think of Alberobello so far?" asked Gianluca, who lived in the area. "It is many things," I began. "The cone buildings are beautiful but don't seem very practical, but then the history makes sense of it. I love the stories behind what we see: avoiding taxes by developing this type of construction, the stories of the man we met, and his memories living in that trullo as a child. Even the stories surrounding the name of this place are interesting, whether its origin is the tree of war or the beautiful tree." My fellow Californian, David, jumped in. "The tourist shops serve a function because the people here have to make a living. Even that is part of their story," he continued, looking in my direction and nodding. "There are a lot of exciting things about this place; I am curious about the symbols on the roofs, some religious, others that refer to a belief in magic.

"Interestingly, they exist side by side, without any problem. Maybe that expresses a bit of the mentality of this place." Gianluca and the others nodded.

One of our Italian friends, Mario, then joined in the discussion. "My favorite part of Alberobello is right here, on this spot, right now with you. I feel like we are at the heart of this town, a little isolated where the trulli are used as homes. Yes, maybe they are rentals, but still, this spot has the atmosphere of a real town, with its history, people and beliefs. And here we are, with you, my friends, who are part of this place at this moment. This moment is what is most important to me here in Alberobello."

Chapter 5
Two Californians and a Masseria

"Do you want to eat at a masseria tonight?" Edoardo asked us. "That depends," I responded. "What is that?" Edoardo laughed. "It is a farmhouse; it is like a fortified farmhouse. They are all over Puglia, and some of them have been transformed into villas or restaurants; others are in ruins, and others are now luxurious hotels. But we want to bring you to an authentic one. They grow and serve organic food. Do you want to go?" I glanced at my companion David, whose eyes said, "I am hungry."

In typical Puglian style, what started as a dinner for five ended up being for twenty, but that wasn't a problem since it is always an adventure to meet new faces in this magical land. Five of us drove, packed into one car, out into the countryside, in an area where the moon was bright, the fields were green, and the houses were scarce. "How far is it?" I asked after we had been on the road for a short time. "About one hour," Edoardo responded, as he pushed on the gas even deeper as we sped forward on the empty road. Edoardo was, by any definition, a crazy driver, and I found myself gripping the door handle to brace myself should we careen off into one of the fields.

We were the first to arrive at the masseria, which wasn't surprising, given that Edoardo was driving 90 miles an hour to get there. We piled out to stretch our legs as clouds drifted across the moon. We stood in the gravel parking area next to a large old stone house, with red tiles on the roof and a tower on the side. "That tower dates from the 1500s," Edoardo said, pointing up. "All these crops belong to the masseria," he continued, "and there is even a space for campers. All the food here is organic. I think you will like it..." he continued as a car drove up. "Buona sera!" said the occupants, two women and one man, a friend of ours named Stefano. "These are my friends Piera and Serena," he said as we shook hands and exchanged greetings and kisses. A few minutes later, other cars pulled up, and people piled out. We were primarily men, but more women joined us in the parking lot. "The women are lesbians," Stefano whispered in my ear as if that mattered. I looked at him and laughed since he seemed to think he was divulging a deep dark secret. A secret it was not.

We trickled into the restaurant; two Americans and the others were Italians from various parts of Italy. The interior of the masseria was rustic: whitewashed walls, tile floors, long tables covered with butcher paper. It was a perfect atmosphere because it felt authentic.

There was a scramble at the table before we sat down. "Chi parla inglese si siede qui accanto a loro - whoever speaks English, come sit next to them," was said, gesturing in our direction. Though I speak Italian, my companion David did not, so they tried to be accommodating. Since it took a while to organize the seating, the "americani" sat down to start munching on breadsticks. After much dragging of chairs and switching places, we were finally all seated.

"Here, you don't order; they bring you what they have since it is all produced on this farm," Edoardo explained. "That sounds dee-lish," David responded.

We had only been in Italy for a day and a half, and soon, even before the food started to arrive, I began to yawn. "Mark!" friend Matteo called out, wagging his finger at my open mouth. I shrugged.

The servers looked like farm ladies; they soon brought out sizzling plates of appetizers. "Do you want? These are called pittule," Edoardo explained, motioning to a plate piled high with fried pieces of dough. Before we could answer, he spooned some onto our plate. It just looked like fried dough. I lifted one with my fork. It tasted just like it looked: fried dough. I looked around, baffled. Was I missing the sauce, sprinkled cheese, or other flavorings? The others were shoveling these dough bits into their mouths down the table. "How are they?" David asked. I tried another one, just in case I got a bad one the first time. "Tastes like greasy dough to me," I said, munching and swallowing with a gulp of wine. "Mark, you don't like?" Matteo asked. "They're fine," I lied. "I want to save some room for the rest."

Suddenly the rest of the appetizers arrived on big platters: fried meatballs, cheese, fried peppers, and eggplant rolls. The chatter subsided as we served ourselves and started shoveling the food. The meatballs were without sauce but crispy on the outside and flavorful inside. The cheese was also fried; I took a small piece, not knowing what to expect. Red and yellow peppers were served in mounds and were excellent with the fresh farm bread. But my favorite dish, which I couldn't get enough of, were eggplant rolls, called *involtini di melanzane*. They were so delicious that the recipe must be included here.

The filling: ground beef, prosciutto, chopped, fiordilatte (cheese), egg, grated parmesan.

The eggplant: sliced grilled eggplant, cut lengthwise and brushed with olive oil.

The sauce was made from fresh tomatoes, cut-up, basil, scallion, salt, and pepper.

The involtini were rolled up, covered lightly with a light tomato sauce, and filled with the delicious flavors of beef, prosciutto, and cheeses. "The more traditional involtini here," Edoardo began, "are made with mortadella rather than prosciutto and without tomato sauce. But these are good too." I nodded, David nodded, and soon, our table was nodding in unison. "We're going to need another platter of them," I said as graciously as possible, in Matteo's direction. He pointed to the platter of fried dough, which was still not consumed. I shook my head. "No thanks to that; more involtini, please!" He laughed, then said in a loud voice towards the opposite end of the table, "The Americans love the involtini!" There was a cheer while someone noted in our direction, "Good taste!"

The next dish served was also a hit: pitta di patate, cheese, and potato casserole. Made from layers of mashed potatoes, pecorino cheese, fresh tomatoes, onions, black olives, and covered with bread crumbs, it made us call out for more, just like ugly Americans. "More involtini and more pitta, please," the two Californians requested in no uncertain terms as we mopped up our plates with bread.

"Mark!" friend Mauro asked, over the clatter of plates and side conversations. "Teach us something in English!" I looked at David and shrugged. He leaned towards Mauro and said, "Debbie Downer." Mauro turned to me and asked, "Cosa e' Debbie Downer - What is Debbie Downer?" David continued, "Debbie Downer is someone who, when you say what a beautiful day it is, responds that 'Tomorrow it will probably rain.' When you tell them that the food is great here, they say it is not fresh enough. When you tell them that you live near the sea, they respond that it is too windy there…" Mauro interrupted, "Yes, yes, I understand." As Mauro started to look around, we got involved in other conversations. After a minute or two, we overheard Mauro say to Edoardo, sitting next to him, "Edoardo, tu sei Debbie Downer - Edoardo, you are a Debbie Downer." There was a brief silence as that part of the table wrestled with the meaning. "What is Debbie Downer?" one asked the other as if they were the twelve apostles sitting around the table at the Last Supper asking, "Is it I?" Although said in jest, Mauro's statement hit Edoardo hard once translated. "I am NOT a Debbie Downer!" Edoardo replied emphatically. "That was probably not the right phrase to teach them," I said, turning to David. "Why do you say that?" Edoardo continued. The mood was no longer cheerful, but Mauro tried to de-escalate it, reassuring Edoardo that he was joking with new words. It took a few minutes for the normal lively conversation to resume, but eventually, it did; at that point, Mauro turned to us and rolled his eyes. "Maybe we should be careful what we teach them," I whispered to David, who nodded.

Since the food paused, it seemed that the meal was over. The Americani grew quiet as jet lag crept in again, and David began dozing off. "Do you want to go outside and explore a bit while they are finishing?" I suggested. So we both grabbed our jackets, told our companions we would return shortly, and went outside to a beautiful medieval-looking courtyard with a painted wooden donkey cart that looked to be several centuries old. I put my hand on it and wondered how many hands touched that spot over hundreds of years. We looked around at the neatly landscaped area, red-brick pavement, and ancient feel of the place. "It's like being in a different world," I said, as David nodded. "Shall we explore some more while they are organizing the bill?" he asked. I agreed, and we circled to the back of the masseria to see where the crops were grown. After a few minutes, I said, "It's cold," and we went back in.

Entering the dining area, we expected our friends to be on their feet, making their way to the exit but, instead, they were seated as before while the staff was bringing new platters full of food. "I thought the meal was finished," I said in astonishment to the Italians sitting next to us. "Nooooooooooo! Now we have another course!" I laughed while David groaned. "Let's make the best of it," I suggested, as plates were passed down the table, full of typical pasta of Puglia called orecchiette alla leccese, made with tomato and ricotta. Once we Californians had our fill, more platters arrived, full of roasted meats. Not knowing what was coming next, I was unsure how to pace myself. I had mistaken the appetizers as the main dish; was I also mistaking the meat for the main dish? But we ate and chatted while David began to doze off again. I looked down the table at our twenty or so friends and companions. I felt grateful to be here in their midst and be welcomed into their extended family.

"Huh?" David said as he jolted awake. "I was just feeling grateful to be here, even though we're sleepy," I said. "Yeah... grateful..." he said skeptically. He looked down the table at our friends with a perplexed look on his face. "What could they possibly be talking about?" he asked. I looked also. It was true that most of our friends, sitting across from each other at this masseria, saw each other almost every day, yet here they were, chatting up a storm as if they hadn't seen one another in decades. I chuckled and wondered aloud. "The weather? Politics? Vacation plans? I have no idea!" I said. Listening to them a bit more closely, I noticed that they were chatting about more personal things: people they knew in common, how this person or that is doing, how they could organize to do something like this again. The chatter seemed to revolve around people, around relationships, rather than around issues or facts. I nodded to myself, thinking, "That is so cool."

It seemed like hours later that dessert was served: a delicious homemade fruit tart as well as apple fritters. Coffee and bitter liquors were brought after another span that seemed like hours. "These are for digestion, so you must try it," Matteo said, smiling, as he passed us the bottle. I poured a bit into my glass and was pleased with the syrupy taste.

Coffee served. Liquor served. David and I grabbed the handles of our chairs, ready to stand up, climb into the car and then get to bed to sleep off jet lag. We looked down at our friends around the table; nobody else seemed to be in a rush to leave. "Are they trying to make a new record for the Genius Book of World Records?" David asked. After ten more minutes of no movement, we decided to play our Ugly American card, so we stood up. "We still have jet lag," I explained to Matteo when we rose. This action spurred a domino effect, as others began to rise. I gave David a thumbs up.

We were at the last leg of the marathon, and now the goal, getting home and getting to bed, was almost in view. We just needed to cross that finish line.

David and I raced towards the car while our Italian friends strolled out. Once in the parking lot, our companions broke up into pockets of two or three conversation groups. I looked around and laughed; I then looked at David, who was not laughing. Not wanting to build on our Ugly American reputation, we waited by the car, gazed at the stars, and made an effort to enjoy the moment. After about fifteen minutes of chatting in groups, our companions began to make their way to the various cars. We bid everyone a good night, grateful for the time together and also to be heading home to a warm bed. "Thank you for this beautiful experience," we said to our Italian hosts. "Did you like?" they responded. I nodded.

We settled back into the car with the heater on and soft music playing and raced along the straight country roads towards home. Then, suddenly, we made a left turn. "I want to show you something on the way home," Edoardo said. "OK," I said, eyes half-open. About twenty minutes later, we pulled up in front of a Renaissance-style country house. "I want you to see this masseria; it is different from the one where we just were," he said. Preferring to be in bed and not adventurous, I kept my ugly American mouth shut, hopped out of the car, and entered the building. It was a vast complex, room after room with tables and fireplaces, guests and plates full of food, an impressive wooden ceiling with stone floors; it was as if we had just stepped into the 16th century! Wandering through the masseria, I found my resistance wearing down and my sense of wonder increasing. As diners looked up, probably wondering what we were up to, we went from room to room in what seemed like a rustic manor house. There was something both magical and authentic about it that we found intriguing. We became unaware of the passing of time or of the need to get home in this place. "Shall we go?" Edoardo asked. I was surprised that he took the initiative. "I know you are tired," he continued. "Can we walk through one more time?" David asked. So we wandered through, not knowing if or when we would return. A few minutes later, we were piled in the car, dozing off, smiling.

The following day, over a cappuccino, we were able to reflect on our evening. We remembered that our Puglian friends have a different sense of time, community, and how to stay together. Relationships are so meaningful that, even if I spend every day with a person, I still have much to share and communicate in the evening over dinner. Time is for building bonds, and a sense of belonging and community is at the center; everything else is trappings. "Wow, they are real friends! They really care for one another!" David exclaimed. "But next time," I responded, "it can't hurt to bring our car." David nodded emphatically.

Chapter 6
Puglia According to the Pugliesi

What does a Pugliese think of Puglia, and how has this land influenced their lives? Rather than speculating, I asked them.

Can you tell us about your life?

Massimo: "I was born in Lecce and lived here until 2009; from that time, I moved to Rome for 'love'. Now I am a professor, and I teach in Rome."

Gio: "I was born in a town in Puglia near Matera. I lived there until I was nineteen, then I joined the military. Once I retired, I returned here to live in Puglia."

Annalisa: "I am 38 years old, and I was born and raised in Taranto, where I work in a large Italian clothing chain. I have three great passions: traveling, photography, and my beautiful city."

Does a stereotypical Pugliese exist?

Massimo: "I have to say that Puglia has three areas with different characteristics: north, central, and south.

"I can speak of a Pugliese from Salento, the south. Salento is in the extreme southern part of the peninsula and is surrounded by water. On the one hand, this area has been subject to invasions, isolation, and domination by other groups and cultures. Communication with the rest of Italy over the centuries was challenging. Many customs and dialects from the ancient world survive here. For example, there are parts of

Salento where the population speaks a dialect very similar to the ancient Greek language.

"The fundamental characteristics of a Salentino are: hospitable, welcoming, and kind. It is also said that the typical person from Lecce is courteous but false. Perhaps this is true for the upper noble families, but not for the rest of the population."

Gio: "Near Bari, there is a more closed mentality; they are far from the sea, far from tourists, so there is a sense of being stuck. Then I moved to this area, to the Valle d'Itria, where people seem more open. I feel more comfortable here. Perhaps because of tourism, the exchange of ideas and intermingling of cultures."

Annalisa: "One of the traits that Pugliesi share is the attachment to one's homeland. The second trait is the love of good food. For an Apulian, there is no place in the world where you eat better! The third trait is a strong sense of belonging to one's family."

What is vital to a Pugliese?

Massimo: "The home is essential for a Pugliese. The goal of the typical Pugliese is to find a way to create a home for himself and the family."

Gio: "To me, the family is the essential point for a Pugliese. The family has a particular patriarchal structure, and this family unit is essential for someone living here."

Annalisa: "I cannot add to what I just said: family, food, and Puglia!"

What are their positive qualities?

Massimo: "Openness towards others and a sense of hospitality are positive qualities. Negative qualities: those from Lecce are amiable and courteous, but they are not direct. Some say they are not completely sincere because they don't say what they think."

Gio: "Pugliesi are very welcoming; they like to meet new people, they are good people. On the negative side, it takes a long time for a Pugliese to trust you before starting a friendship."

Annalisa: "I think that welcoming others is one of the strongest qualities of someone raised here. One negative quality is that some here do not take care of the environment, but this seems to be changing."

If you could describe life in Puglia, which three words would you use?

Massimo: "Home, food, and sea."

Gio: "Peacefulness, simplicity, and humanity."

Annalisa: "My three words for life in Puglia: slow (the rhythms are slower than in the rest of Europe), hot (apart from the meteorological aspect with torrid summers, I mainly refer to human warmth and the sense of welcome), caloric (did I mention the best food in the world?)."

What is the happiest experience you have had in Puglia?

Massimo: "This isn't easy to answer because I've had many happy experiences. What comes to mind is a sunset on the beach in Gallipoli with friends, passing around a bottle of gin, waiting for the sunset; this was a special moment."

Gio: "When I made friends here, the friendships changed my life. The confidence that others had in me helped me to open up."

Annalisa: "The happiest experience was traveling 270 km between the coasts and hinterland of Puglia by bicycle: a slow and intense way of traveling that allowed me to smell scents and look at landscapes in a way that I had never experienced before."

What is the best thing about living in Puglia? What about the worst thing?

Massimo: "The worst thing is finding a job here. The best thing here is the relationships; this is different from my experience in Rome. I know many people in Rome, but I don't have the friendships there that I have found here in Puglia."

Gio: "The worst thing here is, I agree, finding work and being anxious around that. The most beautiful things are the sunsets, climate, and panoramas."

Annalisa: "The best thing about living here for me is the possibility of having a great climate almost all year round, a low cost of living, good food, and luxuriant nature.

"The negative aspects are the economic and administrative ones that we still share with a large part of Italy: the labor system is difficult to access and an excessively complex bureaucracy."

If you were offered a lot of money to leave Puglia forever and never return, would you do that? Why or why not?

Massimo: "I would never make this exchange because I am attached to my land. Puglia is part of me, and I would not exchange this for anything."

Gio: "My land is full of affection and meaningful relationships, and I would never exchange anything for this land."

Annalisa: "I could never leave my land, never to return. Not even for a lot of money. It would be like losing an arm or a leg. We still live without it, but the quality of life deteriorates considerably."

What does a Pugliese think of, say, someone from northern Italy? Stereotypes?

Massimo: "In the eyes of someone from Salento, someone from the north can be seen as one who doesn't know how to live, eat or have friends. I'm not saying everyone from the north is like that, but this is our stereotype."

Gio: "I lived in the north, so I saw many people focussed on earning and getting ahead. They don't enjoy meals and companionship as much as we do."

Annalisa: "Maybe people from the north are always in a hurry and don't know how to relax and enjoy life? But certainly not everyone."

Describe the religiosity in Puglia please.

Massimo: "Religion and faith are felt deeply in Puglia. Perhaps less in the younger generation, but a solid religious tradition is still profound here. I remember my grandparents' attachment to certain religious rites tied to food and culture. Now some of this is being lost.

"In the past, the church was a form of identity for the people. Churches expressed the identity of a group and a sense of belonging.

"But today, these churches are seen as artistic expressions rather than a center of religiosity."

Gio: "I grew up in a very religious family, but my Catholic identity has gone slightly by the wayside. I feel it as part of my background, but I don't live this faith connection as much as before.

"The beautiful churches you see give us a sense of history and belonging."

Annalisa: "Religion in Puglia is a fundamental element and inextricably linked to this land and its culture. Just think of the infinite variety of processions and patronal feasts that take place all year round in the Apulian territory! An example is the Rites of Holy Week in Taranto, which dates to the eighteenth century."

What are your hopes and dreams?

Massimo: "I am seeing that Puglia is becoming more and more well known. When I speak about my city, Lecce, when I am in Rome, the reaction is always 'How beautiful! Stupendous!' Before, no one had ever heard of Lecce!

"I hope this translates into a growth in jobs and the tourist industry."

Gio: "I hope that there are more opportunities for young people to find work and have a career here because many young people leave this area to find a job."

Annalisa: "My hopes concern my city, Taranto, which, unfortunately, has fallen behind the rest of Salento despite the centuries of cultural and historical heritage to offer. My dream would be to participate in this enhancement, to become an ambassador of the beauty of this place!"

What is your favorite thing or place in Puglia and why?

Gio: "Salento gives me a sense of well-being: the colors, the sunsets, the beaches. I rediscovered Salento as an adult, and this gives me a sense of comfort."

Massimo: "Many places are my favorites, but I like this area, the Valle d'Itria. I would probably miss the sea, but I love the panoramas here. I would love to live in a trullo, an ancient stone house."

Annalisa: "Puglia is a unique place in the world. There is no other that brings together culture, art, nature, climate, hospitality, food, and history in this way. Puglia is home; it is the green of the meadows and blue of the sea, the white sand of the beaches, and the rocks in the ravines. It is freshwater from the aquifers and saltwater from the Mediterranean. It is the white of the trulli and the yellow of the wheat. One cannot but love. It cannot leave you indifferent.

"My favorite place in Puglia is wherever I have the sea in front of me. And also the beauty of my city that exudes ancient history. There is nothing like this region."

Chapter 7
Revolutionary in Otranto

Between 1163 and 1165 CE, a monk named Panteleone created the mosaic floor of the cathedral of Otranto. The mosaic contains about 600,000 pieces of stone and covers almost the entire church floor or 700 square feet. The story begins a thousand years ago when two men, one a bishop and the other the abbot of the local monastery, met outside the town of Otranto.

"What year is it?" Bishop Gionata asked the man standing in front of him in an irritated tone. "It is 1161 of Our Lord," Abbot Adeodatus, dressed in the black monk's robes of the Basilian order responded, with a slight bow. "And we still have a cathedral that cannot function. I've heard of churches without roofs, but ours doesn't have windows or altars; it doesn't even have a floor! What are we going to do about this? Can you help me?" Adeodatus looked up at the bishop, sizing him up, deciding how to respond. "If you are looking for donations, this is a poor monastery, and we exist on very little. But if you seek craftsmen and artisans, those we have in our community." The bishop nodded as the tension in the room decreased.

Adeodatus invited the bishop to sit to discuss the situation further. "You have the greatest library in these lands," the bishop began, switching from Greek to Latin. "You have manuscripts in Latin and Greek; scholars come from all the world to study here; your monks transcribe manuscripts for kings and popes. Can not this treasure of knowledge here produce something truly great for our cathedral?" the bishop asked imploringly. Adeodatus put his finger on his lips as he pondered the proposition. The monastery of St. Nicholas of Casole, with 42 monks including the abbot, was a center of learning but not of wealth, and he wanted to be sure that the bishop was truly seeking artisans and not money. "Just what exactly do you have in mind?" Adeodatus asked. Bishop Gionata looked up to think as if seeing an invisible structure above the abbot's head. "I have in mind something... that has never been done before. Something that will make our cathedral great, something that will draw heaven to this place and draw this place to heaven." He looked down into Adeodatus' eyes. "That is all I can tell you. Can you propose this to your brothers?" he asked. Fixed by his gaze, Adeodatus could not refuse. "I will speak with the brothers," he said as he rose with the bishop. "Can you supply me with the plans of the cathedral?" the abbot asked. Gionata smiled. "You will have them in your hands tomorrow," he responded.

The library was quiet, with only the sound of a quill scratching across parchment as one of the monks worked on copying a manuscript. Two others were reading, and a third was browsing the collection. It was true that the monastic library was renowned in all of southern Italy and had been an important center of learning for as long as the monks could remember. Besides farming, the monastery supported itself by copying and producing manuscripts made to order by wealthy patrons or other learning centers. It was necessary to care for the precious manuscripts and know their contents so that visitors and scholars were not obliged to ruffle through the books and scrolls in search of what they were seeking. The librarian of St. Nicholas' role was second in importance only to the abbot. Anthony, the monk in charge of the library, was startled when Adeodatus entered and called him for a private meeting.

Anthony was tall, thin, and pale, made more for parchments than manual labor; he was grateful, so many years ago when the abbot offered him his position. He had built up the library's collections by cultivating relationships with other monasteries and important families, convincing them that his abbey was the safest place to keep their precious writings. An entire book would cost more than a laborer could earn in a year and so was considered a luxury item that could be subject to robbery or disintegration over time. Anthony, therefore, took his job extremely seriously.

"I have something to discuss with you which must remain between us for the moment," the abbot began as the two black robed monks left the library and began to walk across the gardens and away from the buildings. "The bishop has come to me with a request that we aid him in the construction of the cathedral," Adeodatus began. "He is leaving it up to us to choose which project to take on, there being so many." Anthony glanced at the abbot, wondering what this had to do with him. "I need one of our brothers to take on this task; a brother who is learned, energetic and diplomatic. The first monk I thought of was you, Anthony, but this would require you to leave your library responsibilities for someone else since you would be at the cathedral all day, apart from our prayer. What do you say to this?" he asked. Distress passed over Anthony's face, and the abbot read his mind immediately. "Or if you could suggest another if you do not feel fit?" Anthony nodded. "A younger man is needed for this work, one who will not tire as I do..." The abbot nodded. "Bishop Gionata wants the work that we contribute to be great, that will make his diocese, and our monastery, known in all the lands. Can you think of one of our brothers capable of this?" Anthony didn't need to pause. "I can. Panteleone is the man!"

The abbot gazed at Anthony, wondering if he was joking. "Yes, he is a bit of a rebel, and some may even think of him as strange. But there is no one else with more passion for learning and the arts than Panteleone!" Adeodatus chuckled. "Yes, he neglects his work to either read most of the day or to wander the countryside or stare at decaying frescoes in churches. When I asked him where he had been all afternoon, he replied, 'In God's house.' I couldn't get any other explanation from him, but from reports, I know that he goes to the woods and scrutinizes trees, to the river and stares at the water, and I can't tell you how many times I have been told that he leaves his quarters in the middle of the night and looks up at the stars! He is peculiar, yet you say he is the man. Why?" Anthony paused and put his finger on his chin to reflect. "Because he is the only one here capable of creating something unique." The abbot nodded and thanked Anthony.

After the monks had concluded mid-morning prayer in their church, abbot Adeodatus sought out Panteleone. "He disappeared after Matins; he didn't even take breakfast!" one monk told the inquiring abbot. Adeodatus shook his head and turned, adding over his shoulder, "If you see him, please inform me," and he left.

"He is here! He is here in the library!" the tattling monk called out as he knocked on the abbot's door later that day. Adeodatus rose from his small desk and walked across the sunny courtyard into the library area. Once inside, he spotted several of the brothers working on copying manuscripts. In a corner, at a small table, sat a short, stocky, dark-haired bearded man, dressed in the monk's black tunic, studying something on the table. As the abbot approached, he noted that the copying materials were laid to one side while the monk, instead, was turning over specimens of leaves and flower petals that he had laid in rows on the table. As he compared the structure of one leaf to another, he didn't hear the abbot until he stood right next to him. "Panteleone, brother, can you please come to see me in my quarters?" Panteleone looked up and smiled; he had a happy disposition that some regarded as foolishness. He rose from his chair without a word, made a slight bow to the abbot, and followed him out of the library.

The sun was so bright that it made the two men squint as they walked across the cloister, past the gurgling fountain, and through the rows of flowers. Before they reached the abbot's room, Adeodatus paused, turned, and asked Panteleone if they could chat outside. "It is such a beautiful day, and God's creation is inviting us," he said. Panteleone nodded, and the two men, side by side, left the monastery gates and headed towards the countryside.

"Have I done something wrong, Your Excellency?" Panteleone asked, taking the lead in the conversation. Adeodatus chuckled. "No, my son. Nothing at all, so be at peace. But please do not call me excellency; let's reserve that title for the bishop. It is about the bishop that I wanted to speak to you." At this, the abbot recounted the entire conversation he had with Bishop Gionata. Panteleone looked perplexed. "But what does this have to do with me?" he asked, stopping on the path. The abbot turned to look at his questioning eyes. "Because it is you, my son, who has been chosen to create something great for the cathedral, something that will honor God, impress the bishop, and draw people from far away lands to marvel at this church." Panteleone laughed, thinking that this was in jest; his smile faded, however, as he looked up at the severe expression of Adeodatus. "But…" Panteleone began, but the abbot interrupted him. "No 'but,' you can do this, and the Lord will do the rest. I am sure of it. Now, I do not want you to be troubled about this. This task is something that you are called to do; how you will do it and what you will create will manifest itself." Panteleone, with his dark black eyes, stood staring at Adeodatus, drinking in every word. The two stood on the edge of a field, with a wooded area on one side and the distant monastery on the other. Birds were chirping, and there was a brook babbling behind the trees. "The first thing for you to decide," began Adeodatus, "is where you will derive your inspiration from." Panteleone smiled. "Oh, I already know that!" he replied. The abbot cocked his head to one side, inquisitively. Panteleone continued, "The inspiration for this magnificent piece will come from the library… and from this place where we are standing right now."

"Reflect on this for now," Adeodatus said, "but be sure and return to the monastery for mid-afternoon prayer." Panteleone nodded, but the abbot could see that his mind was already somewhere else.

A few days went by before they spoke again. "Shall we visit the cathedral after morning prayer?" the abbot asked Panteleone outside the chapel. The monk nodded and smiled; the two took their respective places as the chanting began.

It was midmorning when they arrived at the cathedral; they found the bishop standing in the middle of the nave, looking up with a dissatisfied expression, shaking his head. But when he saw the two monks approaching, his frown turned into a smile, and he rushed to meet them.

Panteleone was a shy man, and when Adeodatus introduced him, he bowed to the bishop but kept his eyes lowered. Gionata looked him up and down: a stocky, bearded man who appeared strong, shorter than the abbot, with short black, cropped hair and a darker complexion, perhaps of Greek origin. The bishop addressed him in Greek, asking, "What do you think of our church?" Panteleone looked up, first at the bishop, then at the nave, the ceiling, the walls, and the places where windows would be installed someday. He turned in a circle as his dark eyes sparkled. "It is marvelous!" he said. The bishop laughed. "To me, it is an empty shell in need of so much work! What do you see?" he asked the monk. There was a pause; Panteleone continued to look up towards the ceiling as he whispered, "I see what it will be, and it takes my breath away!" The bishop caught the eye of the abbot and gave him a slight nod.

"...he didn't show up for his kitchen duties," Brother Joseph whispered, "so I had to prepare the fish by myself! The man is so forgetful! The bishop is going to be so mad when he discovers that Panteleone has done nothing for him, nothing at all!" The two gossiping monks chuckled. "Do you know where I finally found him? He was sitting on a rock in a field, staring at a tree! Sometimes I think he is mad! When I called him, he just turned to me and smiled, the fool! He had no idea that he had kitchen duties, and..." The two men suddenly stopped as the abbot approached. "Good morning. Is everything well?" Adeodatus asked. The two monks bowed slightly. Brother Joseph spoke first. "I am a little concerned that our brother Panteleone spends much time in the forest or reading secular books and neglects his work for the bishop." The abbot nodded but said nothing; the other monk shrugged. Without saying a word, Adeodatus bowed and left.

Later that afternoon, the abbot found Panteleone in the library and sat down across from him. "What are you reading, son?" he asked. Panteleone smiled and handed him the text. The Golden Ass (Asinus aureus) by Apuleius was the title; Adeodatus frowned. "But this book is about magic and spells, all coming from the demon! Why are you reading this pagan tale?" Panteleone accepted the book back from the abbot. "It is a tale of all those episodes and challenges that each man, and woman, pass through. Some are transformed into beasts by the way they live, others into angels; the rest of us fall somewhere in between. But in the end, just as in this work, there is the hope of redemption. We all hope for this, do we not, abbot?" Adeodatus looked into Panteleone's dark eyes and saw no guile, only sincerity, and a particular curiosity. The abbot nodded and continued, "Have you made progress on the Cathedral project, Panteleone?" "Progress?" the monk responded. "It is almost completed," he said, much to Adeodatus' surprise. "Well, what is it? Where is it?" Panteleone smiled. "It is in my head, and I will sketch it out and hand it to you once it is complete." "But…" Adeodatus started to say but then stopped himself. He looked up to reflect on the words he would choose, but when he looked across at Panteleone, the monk was again absorbed in his book.

"What is your monk imagining?" Bishop Gionata asked the abbot as they conversed in the monastery receiving room. The abbot, Adeodatus, poured a glass of liquor with bitters and handed it to the bishop. "He says the project is almost finished, in his head!" The abbot smiled. "Panteleone is a good man, not a great monk, but he loves his God as he imagines Him, and loves his brothers, as he imagines them also!" The two chuckled. "Would you call him in so we can confer? Maybe he will give me a clue." Adeodatus nodded, opened the door, and asked one of the brothers to fetch Panteleone. "He is either in the library or at the edge of the forest," he added.

A light knock was heard at the door a few minutes later. "Enter," the abbot said in Greek. The door opened slightly, and the stocky, bearded monk, smiling, entered; he bowed slightly to the bishop first and then to the abbot. "Panteleone, Bishop Gionata would like to hear how the project is going. "It is going very well, Your Excellency. It is almost finished." The bishop looked the monk up and down; from his appearance, Panteleone didn't look like an educated man but seemed built more for hauling timber than studying. But obviously, appearances do deceive. "Can you give me an idea? What are you planning? A stained glass window? A fresco? A crucifix?" Panteleone looked down as if seeing an image. "No, these are too lofty for me, Your Excellency." "Then," the bishop continued, "what are you planning to create? What marvelous work of art do you have in your mind?" Panteleone looked up and responded, "The floor." The bishop's jaw dropped open, and he looked over at the abbot, incredulous. "Did I hear him correctly?" Gionata asked the abbot. "I believe so, Your Excellency. The floor."

"It is ready," were the only words written on the note slipped under the abbot's door a few weeks later. Adeodatus immediately knew what it meant and sent word to the bishop. "Come to the cathedral in the afternoon," was the reply, so he alerted Panteleone to be ready. "You have the sketch?" he asked the smiling monk. Panteolone nodded. "May I see it?" he asked. Panteleone's smile faded. "I prefer to show it to you in situ, in the cathedral itself." Adeodatus was curious but respected this mysterious man. "I am looking forward to seeing the fruit of your labors," he said; the monk smiled, bowed, and returned to the library.

The abbot felt nervous as the two made their way to the cathedral, wondering what this young monk would reveal and how the bishop would react. "Why have you decided to decorate the floor rather than a window or wall? His excellency would be happier if you would choose a part of the church that was more visible." Panteleone, the scroll under his arm, continued to walk and look ahead, nodding. "He may be happier this week or this month, but the creation of this floor will resound to eternity," he replied. "Can you not give me an idea? What is depicted? Is it the life of a saint, such as St. Basil? Or decorations with colored stones? Or is it…" he began, but Panteleone interrupted him. "No, it is not that. It is something that will embrace the entire world." With this, the two continued in silence.

The bishop was late in arriving, but Panteleone kept his scroll closed in the meantime. "Greetings, brothers!" the bishop said as he hurried into the church through the doorless entrance and across the dirt floor. The abbot kissed his ring while the monk bowed to the bishop. He rubbed his hands in excitement as Panteleone took the scroll from the bench, walked a few paces forward, and, stooping down, unfurled it. The drawing was many feet long when laid out. He moved to the side as Adeodatus and Gionata approached. There was silence for a long time as the two men gazed at the drawing.

"What is this abomination?" the abbot finally said in disgust. "You have included pagan symbols, even pagan stories, and even sorcery on the floor of a church! Why! I should have..." Before he finished his sentence, the bishop stretched out his arm to silence him. He turned to the monk, who stood on the side with tears in his eyes, and beckoned him over. When he reached the bishop's side, Gionata turned to the abbot. "Would you give us a few moments alone, please?" Adeodatus frowned, turned on his heels, and left the church.

Putting his hand on Panteleone's shoulder, the bishop said: "Tell me about your creation. I am not shocked; I am curious. Please." The sincerity shining from Panteleone's eyes was evident. He looked at the bishop, then at his drawing, and began.

"What is the first thing you see, Your Excellency?" the monk asked. "A tree," the bishop responded. "Yes, a tree, because a tree spans the story of salvation, from the Fall in Eden's garden to the tree on which the savior hung. Just as a tree embraces the whole story of our salvation, this floor will embrace all who enter. Let's look at the branches of this tree, Your Excellency. What do you see?" The bishop walked along the edge of the drawing. "Well, I see some scenes I recognize. I see Cain and Abel here and Noah and his arc there. I also see Adam and Eve here driven out of Eden, the Tower of Babel, and I believe that this is Solomon and the Queen of Sheba. Is that right?" Panteleone was smiling and nodding. "Yes, yes. Then what do you see?" The bishop moved to the other side of the drawing; still unable to take it all in, he stood up on a bench. He shook his head. "I will need your help in discerning the other symbols, Panteleone." The monk picked up a stick and stood near his sketch. "These are the signs of the Zodiac, which recalls the heavens. This man is King Arthur, and this other is the Great Alexander. Here are the myths from the Greek world: Samson, Diana, and Atlas. Over there is 'The Golden Ass,' an ancient work in our library. Now in these circles, we find ourselves, mankind. There are twelve circles for the twelve months, and you can see, in the circles, the activities we engage in at each season. Now here are our known beasts, and over here..." Panteleone stopped when he heard the bishop get down off of his bench. "Come here, my son; let us sit together and tell me more about your vision."

The two men sat beneath a hole in the wall that would one day be a stained glass window. Gionata saw that the monk was a gentle man, so he carefully chose his words. "Tell me why you haven't simply designed the life of a saint or simply biblical stories in your design? You have symbols from the Christian and the pagan world, which should be kept separate since Christ has conquered the world." Panteleone smiled. "But that is the point, Your Excellency! There is no division between the Christian and pagan world because Christ conquered this division. He embraces it all; everything is part of that redemption, and everyone and everything finds its place on that tree of life!"

There was a pause. "Give me an example. How does the story of Arthur, which is unknown except to scholars, find a place on this floor? Or the story of, what did you call it, a golden ass?" The bishop chuckled as he said these last words, and Panteleone smiled. "It is the same thing, Your Excellency, the same theme in both stories. Arthur seeks the grail he believes will bring his kingdom peace and prosperity. In the Metamorphoses, known as The Golden Ass, Lucius seeks to master the art of magic and is accidentally transformed into an ass. So he embarks on a long journey, just like Arthur, in which he seeks salvation. Both Arthur and Lucius find a type of salvation that is fully revealed in Christ for us. The longing of Arthur, the seeking of Lucius, the dissatisfaction of Alexander once he conquered the world: what do these have in common? All of these point to the One for whom our heart longs. So there is no pagan or Christian world since we are all made for the same destiny, for Christ. There is a place for everyone on this tree of salvation; this is what I have tried to express in this work."

They sat there for some time, thinking. Soon the abbot returned with a stern look on his face. "Please sit with us for a moment," the bishop requested. He turned, looked at Panteleone, and then looked at the frowning abbot. "This man has the entire universe in his heart. Take good care of him as he begins his work." The bishop rose, bid them both a good day and left.

Panteleone was humming a little tune while the two walked back to the monastery. The monk seemed unaware of the abbot's irritation. "Always in the clouds," Adeodatus thought as they made their way down the dusty road. Years of religious life had taught him to hold his tongue when he was upset or angry, so the two walked along in the hot sun, the one humming, the other fuming, as the monastic church steeple came within sight. Once inside the cloister, the monk bowed to the abbot and headed to the library.

It was a few days later that Adeodatus popped his head inside the library and whispered to Anthony, the librarian, "Come to my quarters after the midday prayer." After looking around and seeing Panteleone on the far side of the library working on his drawings, the abbot shook his head and disappeared.

"We must stop him!" Adeodatus said as soon as Anthony stepped into his quarters. "Stop who? Stop what?" Anthony asked as he sat down across the desk from the abbot. "Stop that mad monk from creating an abomination! Do you know what he is doing? He intends to put pagan symbols on the floor of our cathedral!" Anthony looked at Adeodatus, perplexed. "What does the bishop say?" The abbot rose to his feet. "He supports him! He supports this! But what do you expect!" "Be careful what you say," Anthony interrupted him. Adeodatus was a good man and immediately realized his fault in presuming to judge another man. "I am sorry. I do not understand why he doesn't design the lives of the saints on the pavement! Better yet, why does he not paint a fresco of an episode from the life of Christ on the wall, as in so many churches? Do you know what he intends to put on that floor? Stories from Roman pagans, from the false gods of Greece! He even intends to depict that adulterous story of Arthur, that little-known story from the West! We will be the laughing stock. You, Anthony, are learned, Panteleone respects you; speak to him, convince him to abandon this terrible work!" Anthony sat there looking, his mouth agape. He had never seen the abbot in such a state. He paused, not knowing how to respond. Finally, he rose in silence and, just before leaving, said, "I will speak with our brother."

Panteleone was not in the library when Anthony returned, but his scrolls were still on his table. The librarian was a curious man, so he sat down and unrolled the first scroll where he saw elephants upon whose backs grew a tree. The branches reached out and embraced somewhat cartoonish images, but in them, the librarian recognized depictions of culture, literature, and art housed in his library. He nodded his head as he looked from scroll to scroll, realizing that this monk had captured something unique about this world and the next. He expected Panteleone to enter when the door opened, but another monk came to copy books. Curiosity quickened, Anthony got up and left the building to search for Panteleone. He longed to understand every image on those scrolls, and only Panteleone could enlighten him.

Anthony crossed the field and called out to Panteleone among the trees, but there was no sign. He went to the kitchen, but he wasn't there. "The garden!" he said to himself; he was sure this time, but three other monks were tending the vegetables, not Panteleone. He stood there in the cloister, thinking as the bell began to toll, drawing his attention to the church. He hastened across the garden, into the corridor, and opened the church's back door. As his eyes adjusted to the darkness, he spotted the black-robed monk, standing in the middle of the church, arms outstretched, looking towards the crucifix. Anthony decided to wait and took a seat on the right choir. Minutes passed, and still, this monk didn't budge. Anthony looked at Panteleone's face; the monk was smiling, and he could barely make out the words in Greek that he was whispering: "Ευχαριστώ," "Thank you."

Anthony grew tired, so he withdrew and left the monk to his God.

It was early the next day, after morning prayer, that Panteleone came to the library. "I've been hoping to speak with you," Anthony whispered as the monk passed his desk. Panteleone smiled; he then motioned with his hand and invited the librarian to accompany him to the table where he usually worked, piled high with scrolls and books. Not wanting to admit that he had already looked at the drawings, Anthony began: "I have heard that your designs for the cathedral are complete, and I am most anxious to see them," he said.

Panteleone paused as he considered the request. "The abbot hasn't told me to keep them secret, but I am concerned that the designs may distract the brothers from their monastic life." Anthony was not prepared to take no for an answer. "That is very good of you, brother. I will not speak a word of your work to the others, and perhaps I can be of assistance to you." Panteleone smiled and looked into Anthony's eyes, searching. Believing that the librarian was just as excited about the work, he made a split-second decision and unfurled the first scroll.

The drawings were almost simplistic, something a child would draw, yet depicted things far beyond what children are taught. "What is it?" Anthony asked, eyes wide open. "This is life," Panteleone whispered.

"We are all part of this living tree from which we derive life, meaning, knowledge, fulfillment, and love. We are bound together through this tree, which represents creation." "But," Anthony interrupted, "why does the tree stand on the backs of two beasts rather than on the earth?" Panteleone nodded as he stared at the drawing. "Because the earth is dead: it is dirt and rocks. The tree of life, however, springs from the living." Anthony shot him another question. "Is this Alexander the Great? And this the legend of King Arthur? And these, are not these the gods of the Greeks? And this, what is this? Images of Roman writers? And here, this looks like chess pieces. And over there, signs of the Zodiac. Why? Now I see here, on the other side, are images from our holy Bible: Noah and the flood, the garden of Eden, the tower of Babel, heaven and hell and up here," he continued, pointing, "what is this?" Panteleone squinted and looked. "These are the virtues and vices of men." Anthony interrupted him. "But why? Why place pagan symbols next to Christian truth?" he asked, his eyes wild with interest and wondering. Panteleone was a simple man, and his answer expressed his simplicity: "Because, in the end, there is room for us all."

Just as Anthony opened his mouth to question the monk further, the bell rang for midday prayers, beckoning the brothers to the church in silence. Panteleone stood, rolled up his scrolls, smiled, bowed to the librarian, and left.

Anthony didn't sleep well that night; it was as if the words of Panteleone were burning within. He was relieved when the sun rose, and he made his way into the church to find some peace. As the chanting began, Panteleone slipped in, looked up at the altar with a smile, and joined in. As usual, he was late.

Anthony wondered why the monk's few words perturbed him so much during the prayers. He was much older and more experienced than Panteleone, this young monk had an openness of spirit that he found extraordinary. While some ridiculed Panteleone as a fool and of small intelligence, Anthony was beginning to see otherwise. What did this inexperienced monk understand about life that Anthony had not grasped with all his years of study and service? Perhaps this was the question that perturbed the librarian the most.

Later in the day, Panteleone appeared in the library; his monk's robe was grass-stained and had a flower stuck to it. "Out daydreaming in the woods again," a younger monk whispered to another as he walked by. Arriving at his table, he unfurled his drawings and stood, looking at them, scanning every inch. "Good afternoon, brother," Anthony said, startling Panteleone. "I am sorry for creeping up behind you," Anthony said. Panteleone smiled, then returned to looking at his drawings. "May I not ask you some more questions about your design?" the librarian asked, trying to sound as carefree as possible. The other monk nodded and sat down; Anthony sat across from him.

"Why do you place paganism on the same level as our salvation history in your design? Do you not realize that our abbot is furious about this? How can our Lord be on par with... with... King Arthur, Alexander, or any other persons and things not found in our holy Scriptures? Is this not blasphemous? I want to understand!" Anthony asked, with passion in his tone. Panteleone smiled; he looked at his drawings, then looked into Anthony's eyes. "Does it not say in our Scriptures that all of creation yearns for completion? Is this completion not creation's fulfillment in Him, the Creator, and Destiny of all things? Then why do we have to separate the world into parts, some redeemed, others not? From the ancient world," Panteleone continued, as he gestured to an image of the Huntress Diana, "to our present time," the monk continued, gesturing across the entire drawing, "men have sought the truth, sought happiness and meaning. All of these stories, recorded in the Scriptures or found outside, lead to the same destination: Christ." Panteleone's eyes were sparkling as he said these words, and he looked into Anthony's eyes to see if the librarian grasped his meaning. Anthony took a deep breath. "But this has never been done before! This floor you are proposing will confuse those who see it. They will not grasp its meaning. It is too much for our minds, for the poor peasants who will visit..." He trailed off. Panteleone answered him: "God is not too great for any man."

With these words, Panteleone smiled and concluded, "I have an appointment with the forest. Good day, brother." He rose, bowed at Anthony, then left.

There was a slight knocking on the abbot's door. Looking up from his writing desk, Abbot Adeodatus wondered who it could be in the middle of the afternoon when all the monks were busy. "Enter," he said in Greek. Anthony slipped in and carefully closed the door behind him. "Let me guess," Adeodatus began, "you have come about Panteleone." Anthony smiled while the abbot frowned as he motioned for the librarian to sit. Anthony broke protocol by starting the conversation. "I believe that the work of our brother Panteleone should move forward unimpeded. My reasons for this are threefold. First, Panteleone is a man of faith. Second, his work expresses the universality of salvation. Third, this design expresses all of the knowledge and wisdom of this world." When Adeodatus tried to interrupt, Anthony continued. "Long after our earthly journey is complete, this floor, and what it represents, will remain. This intuition in stone is our chance to leave our mark on history! Only Panteleone, who doesn't fit into any monastic category I have encountered, could have come up with this, Father. You see, I was a skeptic also until I allowed myself to see through his eyes rather than mine. The simplicity of this design yet the complexity of what it expresses! This work is monumental, Father Abbot, and I don't think any of us should stand in the way of Panteleone. I have offered to assist him, should he need it. All of our support will be needed to bring this work from the land of dreams to the pavement of the cathedral. All of our support means from the least monk toiling in the kitchen to you, Father Abbot. Yes, you. I believe that this is God's work, and I ask you, as your fellow monk and brother, to speak with Panteleone and to look at the design from his point of view." There was a pause before the abbot responded. "I will do as you have said." Anthony smiled, bowed, and left him.

It took some days but, after speaking with Panteleone and being hounded by Anthony, the abbot gradually warmed up to Panteleone's vision. "What is it that finally convinced you?" Anthony asked the abbot the following week. "It was a simple statement of our brother Panteleone. With his simple soul, he said 'But Father, there cannot be a contradiction between creation and salvation! He is both the Creator and Savior; He is the same!'" Faced with these words, I could have no more objections.

A few days later, Adeodatus let Bishop Gionata know that the project was ready to move forward; the following week, the work began. Not having the money to employ a complete workforce, the bishop and abbot agreed that the monks would devote their working hours to realizing Panteleone's design. The designer himself acted as the foreman.

Both Anthony and Abbot Adeodatus knew that not all of the brother monks would support the all-encompassing vision that Panteleone wanted to express. To prevent discord, Adeodatus took the authoritarian approach. Calling all the monks to the Chapter meeting, he explained that Bishop Gionata had commissioned their brother Panteleone to design the pavement floor for the cathedral and that the bishop had envisioned the design to be "universal in scope with biblical undertones." He asked the monks to support this work which would mark their town and their monastery as a pilgrimage destination for centuries to come. "Does our brother Panteleone have your support, my brothers?" he asked. The monks looked at one another and glanced at Panteleone, who was looking at his folded hands. The perplexed looks gradually turned into smiles and nods. "Yes," was the answer of the eldest monk, Kleopas.

To transfer the drawing to the floor required mathematical skills to keep the figures in the correct dimensions. Panteleone had devised a system using wooden stakes and rope, crisscrossing the floor, as Anthony assisted him in the measurements. Once he laid the grid, Panteleone used chalk to create a draft of the design to see how it would look on a large surface. It took the monk nearly a week to outline the plan on the concrete base that would serve as the foundation. It was a Monday when the outline was shown to the bishop and the monastic community. As they gathered at the church door, there was silence followed by a gasp of awe. Panteleone was standing behind as his brother monks jostled for a position for a view of the floor. Two monks in front turned to Panteleone; their mouths hung open in shock. They approached the designer as their surprise turned to smiles. One of the monks embraced him and began to weep. "I have never seen anything so beautiful created by the hand of man," he said as his tears wet Panteleone's beard. Soon the other monks gathered around him; each saw this man in a new light. Embarrassed by the attention, Panteleone looked down as each one congratulated him.

"My brothers!" the abbot called to them. "This is just the design with chalk. We have to make it with stone now." Kleopas expressed what all were feeling: "We are ready to begin at once."

The monks were all smiling when they turned to thank the bishop for his support and sponsorship, but when they turned in his direction, Gionata had gone.

The weeks turned into months as Panteleone directed the work and Bishop Gionata traveled across Italy and beyond in search of sponsorship. The first workers were only monks, but local and Norman artisans were employed when the bishop could pay wages. More donations came in when word about the unique floor spread, and Gionata eventually hired artisans from Tuscany.

Panteleone had projected the floor would take one year, which stretched beyond two since work had to stop periodically when donations ran low. The quiet and quirky monk's reputation rose in the monastery as the chalk design became stone, and his vision became not only accepted but celebrated. "I doubted you," the abbot told Panteleone one day in his office. "Now that I see the floor halfway finished, I've come to see it as a window into your soul, my son." At this, Panteleone blushed. "Please don't be ashamed. Somehow, this work has made my soul bigger, if such a thing is possible." Panteleone smiled, glancing up into the abbot's eyes.

Days became months as the chalk design took on the flesh of stone. However, during the last weeks of construction, the monks noticed a phenomenon that disturbed them. Whenever Bishop Gionata spoke of the design on the pavement, he did not refer to Panteleone or their monastery. "My design," or "The concept that I came up with," was how he referred to the work taking shape. Their fears that the monastery's role might be obscured were confirmed one day when, once the date of the unveiling of the floor was set, the bishop asked for a change in design. "I would like my name embedded in the floor itself, in a prominent position." When the abbot referred these words to Panteleone, the monk was saddened. "But the work is not to magnify men," he said. The abbot patted his shoulder. "I know, my son. But I do not think we have a choice." In the days that followed, the desire of Bishop Gionata was carried out; his name was placed in stone.

The year was 1165; the cathedral would be consecrated and the mosaic floor revealed during the Easter services. While the celebration of holy week and the consecration were being planned, a discussion was brewing in the monastery. "But you cannot allow this to happen!" Anthony, the librarian, dared to say to the abbot. "Our brother Panteleone and the entire monastery have worked tirelessly to create this masterpiece! And to have a bishop take all the credit! This is preposterous…!" "Calm, my brother," Abbot Adeodatus protested. "Let's not say anything we may regret. I share your feelings, but I am powerless. He is the bishop and so has sole authority in this area. My authority only reaches to the walls of this abbey." Anthony could not help himself. "Well, cannot we monks do something to stop this?" Adeodatus shook his head. "I cannot sanction any actions against the bishop." The two men stood in the abbot's office, silent. "You said that you cannot sanction any actions, correct?" The abbot nodded. There was a slight smile on the librarian's face as he bowed and took his leave.

After the midday prayers, Anthony whispered in the ears of several of the younger monks. "Meet me at the library; it is urgent!" A few moments later, the librarian and five monks were gathered among the books and scrolls, huddled in the corner outside the earshot of others. Panteleone then entered; the group of monks smiled and bowed at him. Anthony motioned with a slight nod that the plotting monks should go outside while Panteleone sat at his table. "Let us take a stroll in the woods to enjoy God's creation, my brothers," Anthony said loud enough for bystanders to hear. The group then left the monastic grounds, crossed the field, and entered the woods. The scheming began.

It was the middle of the night, on the eve of the consecration, that the group of monks set out, carrying heavy tools and bags of colored stones. Anthony motioned to them to keep silent as they made their way out of the monastic walls. They stealthily walked down the road and up towards the cathedral. The floor was covered when they entered, awaiting the unveiling the next day. Anthony unfurled the modified design, containing the name of Bishop Gionata. "A reference to our Panteleone will accompany every reference to his excellency," Anthony proclaimed in a loud whisper. The monks lit candles, unpacked their tools, and began to hack at the floor, splitting stones and lifting them to replace them with those they had prepared. This entire process only took a few hours. Once finished, the monks seemed satisfied with their work, except for a younger monk named Marius.

"It is not enough," Marius said. "Panteleone should have such a prominent place that all who enter here will see that this is his work. His name should be... here," he said, pointing down near the front entrance. "In large letters, without shame." Anthony objected. "But this will also be the first thing that the bishop sees tomorrow, and he will be angry." Marius shook his head. "The responsibility for the bishop's feelings is his own. We must do what is right. We must honor our brother, whose legacy and monastic community were about to be lost. This is the right thing," Marius said as he took out his sledgehammer. The other monks looked at Anthony for direction. "He is right. Let us proceed," he said.

It took the rest of the night for the group to take out a chunk of the floor, fashion the stone into the letters of the name of Panteleone, level it, sand it, and cover it over again. The first rays of light became visible when Anthony motioned for silence; the monks stood in a circle and prayed, then secretly made their way back to their beloved monastery of St. Nicholas of Casole.

Several monks were sleepy-eyed as the long procession entered the cathedral the following day. Dignitaries streamed in and were seated near the altar as peasants stood in the back and sides. But every last one, from merchants to rulers to priests and prelates, marveled at the work. Those who entered the church found themselves looking down rather than up. Not one missed the prominent signature of the monk who conceived of it all. "Who is this Panteleone?" was the question buzzing through the church before the ceremony began. Some pointed at the simple bearded black-robed monk, walking towards the main altar among his brothers.

At the end of the procession was Bishop Gionata, adorned with gold vestments, crozier, and miter. He blessed the people as he passed, smiling and pleased. As he crossed the threshold, he glanced down and saw the name "Panteleone" in large letters from the corner of his eye. He tripped but caught himself with his crozier as a deacon rushed to his aid. "Are you alright, Your Excellency?" the deacon asked. "I am," replied the bishop, as he clenched his teeth and his smile faded.

The Easter day service, combined with the cathedral's consecration, lasted until early afternoon. Hoping to avoid any open conflicts with the bishop, Abbot Adeodatus ushered his monks quickly back to the monastery where they could celebrate as a monastic community. Several of the brothers congratulated Panteleone as they walked, but the monk was quiet and seemed embarrassed by his new celebrity. Upon entering the monastic enclosure, tables and chairs had been moved outside where a feast was being prepared. The smell of roasting meat filled the air. "In one hour, we will serve," the monk cook proclaimed as the other monks filed past. Anthony stood by the end of one of the tables, smiling as he thought of the long road that had brought them to this point. The abbot startled him when he approached him from behind, whispering, "Do you know anything about how the name of Panteleone appeared on the floor of the cathedral? You know that the bishop will demand answers." Anthony looked at the abbot and sought to respond but realized that any response would complicate the situation. So he bowed to the abbot and fled to the church, where he awaited the bell for the meal.

The feast began without the usual silence and reading; the monks chatted, laughed, and rejoiced that their long toil to bring the design to fruition reached completion. "But I do not understand," Panteleone said to the brother sitting next to him, "how my name appeared on the pavement." The monk next to him smiled and replied, "I do not know how your name appeared, Panteleone, but I do know why. It is because your brothers here love you."

Suddenly, there was a loud knocking at the monastic enclosure's front gate, and all grew silent. The brother in charge of the door rushed over and peaked outside; he was chatting with an unknown person. He then shut the door, approached the abbot, and whispered in his ear. The abbot smiled and rose. "Arise, my brothers," he said. "Panteleone, come here with me, please," he said. Panteleone blushed, got up, and hurried beside the abbot; the entire entourage then approached the gate, which opened with a push of the hand of the brother. The monks gasped as they looked out to see the whole town gathered in front of them, headed by dignitaries, visiting bishops, and noble families, all wanting to meet the monk who was the creator of this work. The abbot walked Panteleone to the front; the monk was now red as a beet. He bowed to the people, and they broke out singing. The dignitaries came forward and shook his hand; the visiting bishops came and embraced him, the people proclaimed him.

A few moments later, Bishop Gionata appeared from the side. He stood from a distance and watched the scene as the townspeople and prelates showed gratitude to a man who wanted to remain in the background. The more he gazed at the people and the reaction of this monk, the more he felt moved. As he watched the face of Panteleone, blushed with eyes cast down, something began to happen to Bishop Gionata. Tears welled up in his eyes; the coldness with which he had grasped for fame began to melt.

Almost unconsciously, he began to walk.

All eyes were on him as he approached Panteleone; the bishop bowed and kissed the hand of the monk as the people erupted in cheers.

The dream of Panteleone had become a reality. There was room enough for all.

Chapter 8
Jingle Bells Rock and a Living Nativity

"Do you want to go see a living Nativity scene?" our Pugliesi friends asked one brisk late December morning at our airbnb in Lecce. We must have looked baffled because Matteo continued: "It's a tradition that started in Assisi, with St. Francis. You should experience it! He was the first to gather a donkey, a few sheep, cows, and village people of Greccio to reenact the first Nativity."

Francis lived in the 1200s, an era of division and power jostling and a Church culture more based on a class system than Gospel values. Francis became a victim in the division, having been kidnapped for ransom by authorities in Perugia; after his release, he had a conversion experience in which he embraced "Lady Poverty" and sought to live his life in imitation of Christ.

During this time, Francis noticed that there was a lot of preaching and discussion about the divinity of Christ but little reference to his humanity. God seemed far away from human affairs and concerns; religiosity came to consist of rituals observed with one's daily life unaffected. This situation didn't work for Francis. His experience was that God either entered the here and now or had nothing to do with human concerns. So he began to live his life as if the only thing that mattered was his relationship with the Christ he believed in.

Before Christmas in 1223, Francis was pondering how the birth of Christ might be experienced as an encounter with a person rather than regulated to the field of theological principles. Having visited Nazareth, Francis brought this memory back with him as he went from house to farm, asking the town to help recreate the Nativity of that first night. A contemporary of Francis, St. Bonaventure (1221 - 1274), wrote:

"Then he prepared a manger and brought hay, an ox, and an ass to the appointed place. The brethren were summoned, the people ran together, the forest resounded with their voices, and that venerable night was made glorious by many brilliant lights and sonorous psalms of praise."

The scene was set up in a cave right outside the town of Greccio; St. Bonaventure goes on to write about that night:

"The man of God [St. Francis] stood before the manger, full of devotion and piety, bathed in tears and radiant with joy; the Holy Gospel was chanted by Francis, the Levite of Christ. Then he preached to the people around the Nativity of the poor King, and being unable to utter His name for the tenderness of His love, he called Him the Babe of Bethlehem."

This emotional scene moved the people so much that the practice spread to other towns; this tradition is still kept today in some parts of Italy.

With these images in mind, we all piled in a car and drove to a village in Puglia where there was the most well-known and frequented live Nativity scene, according to our local friends.

I was giddy with anticipation.

Christmas had already come and gone, but the living Nativity was operating until January 6, the feast of the three kings. When our car approached the area, we saw a police officer directing traffic; it seemed like a mob had descended on that place. Quick judgment enabled us to make a left turn into a supermarket parking lot, where we used the portapotty and were then ready for our Nativity experience.

The first thing I noticed was the music. I expected the soft Christmas carols of my youth, but Mariah Carey's *Christmas* album was blaring from speakers set up everywhere. By the time we made our way to the front entrance, Julio Iglesias' *Feliz Navid* was blasting in my ear from the nearby speaker. Since our Pugliesi friends didn't react, we Californians limited ourselves to rolling our eyes.

The line snaked around the path and into the street. "Is there an admission fee?" I asked. "Donations only, but we should give something," was the response. I nodded as I looked up the path towards an entrance that looked like the front gate into a zoo on the right, an algae-filled pond on the left. "I'm not going to be judgmental; I'm going to be open to experiencing this," I said to my brain.

A boat with two teenagers was in the algae pond, dressed in costumes resembling ancient villagers, with fake fishing poles, drifting and smiling. A woman with a large basket full of 5 and 10 euro bills was also there; the donation seemed like an entry fee, so I obliged and dropped in my cash. With Mariah blasting again, we passed out of the crowd and into the small road constituting the loop that would take us through the temporary village.

Small shops were lining the road, constructed from wood and painted to appear old. We ducked into the first one where a woman and her daughter, dressed in tattered villagers' clothing, were kneading and mixing dough. I was hungry and waiting around to, hopefully, get a sample, but there didn't seem to be any product coming out. It was just for show. I nodded and looked at my partner David; he nodded back, and we left.

As we made our way around the road's curves, we noticed that some shops were simple demonstrations of what life might have been like in ancient Nazareth, whereas others had artisans displaying their wares. We came across a woodcarver intent on his craft; occasionally, he glanced up at us gawkers. He was a handsome man in his 40s; samples of his carvings and his business cards were near the entrance to the shop. We proceeded to the following few shops until we heard "Where are Mario and Enrico?", members of our party. We stopped and looked around, but the two had disappeared. After waiting a few moments on the road, Matteo, one of our Pugliesi friends, went to look for them. We grew restless and began to wander further since the road sloped upwards towards the top of the hill. Matteo caught up with us later and exclaimed, "They're still at the carver's shop, staring at that beautiful woodcarver!" he said, laughing. "Let's move on," he suggested.

Suddenly we found ourselves in a massive line of people, waiting to get to the outdoor counter of an old shack; we had no idea what was inside, but we were trapped. "We can see when we get up there," I suggested. But the line was hardly moving. I spied that some were being handed some free food wrapped in paper and were munching as they left the shop window. "What is it?" David asked. I repeated the question to our Pugliese friend, Matteo. "Struffoli," he said. Not knowing what it was, I got out of line to look closer, then returned to our small group. I told David in English: "It's those fried balls rolled in sugar. Do you want to wait in line for that?" Without skipping a beat, his reply was swift and decisive. "I'm not eating that shit!" We both got out of line, and the others followed.

Soon the others showed up. "How did it go?" I asked. "Good. We were able to chat with him about possibly doing some business together," Mario replied. Matteo rolled his eyes. "Business! Fammi un favore," which loosely means "Give me a break!"

As Jingle Bell Rock rang out from the speakers, we continued our journey among the crowds. "But where is the nativity scene?" I asked in a somewhat whiney voice. "This is all the nativity scene," was the answer. So I repeated to my brain: "Don't judge, just observe and enjoy." Though my brain objected, I kept my mouth shut.

We then entered into a structure decorated to resemble a palace where a teenager was seated on a throne with two guards on each side. "King Herod," I read out loud, from the sign, as the self-conscious youth fidgeted as we filed past.

We went on to gawk at the shop with the candle maker, the ironworkers, and the basket weavers as we approached the "synagogue," populated by more teenagers dressed in robes standing around a table with a menorah and book representing the Torah on it. The corny costumes and fidgeting teenage actors were part of the charm. Some visitors were taking photos while we paused and looked around. I felt my heart soften and some of my earlier cynicism fade as I realized that this event was an effort by the whole town to represent events that carry so much meaning. I smiled as we left.

We then entered the house of the Romans, where several young people dressed as soldiers with red capes stood guard. Another group of "soldiers" entered to start their shift. They laughed and joked, some wearing only part of their costumes, revealing blue jeans and t-shirts. As we passed them and approached a wooden bridge, I again smiled, thinking of my students back in California.

Our path led us to a slightly more isolated part of this Bethlehem.

Frosty the Snowman kicked in over the loudspeakers; I couldn't help giving our group a curious look. Matteo, reading my thoughts, shrugged. "Now, where are we headed?" I asked. "To see the Nativity scene, straight ahead," he responded. I looked forward to this stop since it would culminate our visit and was the reason for all the activity.

After crossing the bridge, we headed towards a wooden hut with a straw roof, where visitors were gathered outside the door.

We entered the dim room, with some yellow lights on the sides hidden by hay, with one light shining on the three figures in the center. Joseph seemed to be more of a grandfather and Mary more of a teenager, but the baby was real (not a doll). It was a borrowed baby since there didn't seem to be a bond between the Mary figure and baby, but we stood there and gawked, all the same. No words were said by either the actors or the spectators; it was as if everyone felt like they were in a church. The music from outside was muffled, the atmosphere inside was self-conscious but cozy; it was a refuge from Frosty and Mariah and Iglesias, so I wanted to linger. "We should go," my friends said as the crowd started to push us through.

As we exited the scene, we immediately found ourselves in the more commercial area: a gift shop, snack bar, and sit-down restaurant on top of the hill. The music was blasting again, the coziness disappeared, and we were back in the Christmas atmosphere from which Charlie Brown longed to be liberated. As I took one last look down the hill, along the winding street with shops and village actors, I wondered if this tradition had started as a quaint or spiritual tradition and then had become... this. I asked David what he thought, but he whispered, "Let's not criticize this; the Italians brought us all the way here, and they might get hurt!" He was right; I didn't want to judge but only be present.

"There are more authentic Nativity scenes than this one," Mario said in an apologetic tone as we made our way down the hill. "I would love to see one of those next time," I responded.

As we got in the car to make our way home, I reflected on the experience. A nativity scene was supposed to be quiet, focussed, and spiritual, just like the first Christmas I envisioned. After walking up the shop-lined road, the scene at the end seemed to be the most ignored and least important area. Shopkeepers were busy demonstrating their skills, networking with future customers, teenagers dressed in costumes cavorting with their friends, tourists gawking and taking photos, and most everybody was munching on something. And the blaring music! "This wasn't the way it was supposed to be!" I thought as we drove off.

After dwelling on these thoughts and judging the village somewhat harshly for commercializing Christmas, it struck me that the very unimportance of the nativity scene at the end was the most authentic part of our adventure. There were shopkeepers doing business, just like that first Christmas. Hotel owners, travelers, and workers hurrying to get home for dinner. Restaurants were serving, diners eating, teenagers laughing, mothers scolding, shepherds watching, soldiers lounging, and children sleeping. It was just like that first Christmas when, in a hidden corner of the town, completely ignored by its inhabitants who were focussed on their own lives, a baby was born that would turn the course of history.

So my cynicism gave way to the realization that, without even trying, this town had managed to create a Christmas scene just like that first one in Bethlehem.

Chapter 9
Dancing in Nardo'

"Tonight we go to Nardo' to see La Pizzica, a traditional dance in Puglia that tells a story. Do you want to come? There is a restaurant where the food is good, and the performance is authentic. No tourists, except us. Do you like?" Our friend Mario looked intensely at us, hoping for an affirmative answer. "That sounds exciting. Yes. But will we understand it?" I responded. Mario nodded. "We will explain there. I think you will love it." The matter was settled.

It was already dark when we piled into the car for the short drive to Nardo'. "How many of us will be there?" I asked. Mario paused as he counted in his head. "Eight, I believe." I nodded, not surprised that the group had grown from three to eight. "Before we arrive," our other friend Mauro began, "I want to tell you the origins of this dance."

"Even before the Roman Empire, this area was populated by Greek colonies, and you can even hear some influence of the Greek language in the dialects. Southern Italy has many ruins of temples of Greek origin, like Paestum, for example. So La Pizzica derives from a family of dance traditions named after a tarantula spider. I will explain that part later, but, for now, think about the ancient Greeks who lived here. They had their customs, their culture, their religions, and traditions. One of the most famous Greek gods was Dionysus, who is now known as the god of wine. But he was also connected to anger and joy since wine can affect you both ways. Unlike other gods, the primary way that the Greeks worshiped him was not in temples but in wooded, hidden areas. His followers were called Maenads, who were almost like wild women. They would accompany Dionysus into the forests; they were dressed with the skins of fawns and carried rods tipped with pine cones. These women would dance and go into a sort of madness or ecstasy. Some historians claim that if these frenzied followers came upon an animal, they would rip it apart and eat its flesh raw, believing that they would take on that animal's powers.

"So, honoring Dionysus felt very liberating for these women followers. There were no constraints, no men telling them what they could or could not do. They could be as uninhibited as they wanted to be, and they expressed their freedom and wildness in their dance. From this tradition derives the Tarantula from which La Pizzica, which we will see tonight, evolved." Just as he completed this sentence, our car pulled up next to another; we parked and found our companions waiting for us.

"Are you ready to dance the Pizzica?" Matteo asked us playfully. He then grabbed a kleenex and started to twirl and move his hips seductively. Another companion, Gianni, joined in, and soon the two were circling one another and performing comical dance moves in the parking lot. When another car drove up and parked, they stopped. We laughed.

When we entered the restaurant, lively music was already going strong, with young men dressed in traditional garb playing the accordion, guitar, tambourine, castanets (clappers), and a fife (a type of piccolo). The atmosphere was festive and crowded with children, grandmothers, and everything in between. Our large table was in the corner next to the band. When we arrived, we discovered some friends were already seated. Somehow we managed to get twelve around that table. Mauro sat next to us to give us a running narration.

Soon the wine was flowing, and the clatter of plates diverted our attention from the entertainment to our table. "This is a pasta that is typical of Lecce," Mauro began. "Notice that it is shaped like ribbons; it imitates the baroque architecture that you find in the city." As he was speaking, more plates of *sagne cannulate* were served:

long ribbon pasta covered with a mild tomato sauce that tasted so fresh it seemed to be still on the vine. Soon afterward, large platters of steaming chicory with fava beans, followed by mountains of fried meatballs. The meatballs were without sauce, but their tenderness and subtle herb flavorings made sauce superfluous. We ate and chatted as the music played in the background. The sense of expectation increased through our meal, while platters were carried out of the kitchen and deposited on the twenty or so tables within the restaurant.

Suddenly the music died down, and a beautiful woman appeared, holding a long scarf and wearing a red dress. She almost looked Spanish, with her flowing traditional garb and hair pulled back. Mauro whispered in my ear: "Now she is asking for a companion to dance the Pizzica with her. Do you want to?" I shook my head. Surprisingly, after a short pause, a man from a nearby table, in his thirties, rose to his feet, approached her, and bowed. The dance could now begin.

"As I said before, the dance you will see," Mauro began again, "is part of a group of dances called The Tarantula. The origins are in the fourteenth century, during which time it was believed that if a spider or scorpion bit someone, this frenetic dancing would free them of the poison. The principal instruments are the violin and tambourine because of the combination of rhythm and melody. They saw this frenetic music as a type of exorcism that would free the woman of the poison. This music might have been played for days or even weeks to drive the evil away. In those ancient musical rites, they sought to arouse all the senses, to drive the poison away, including brightly colored blankets, scarves, and ribbons. They stimulated the sense of smell using cedar, geraniums, and basil. So they believed that this exhilaration would drive the evil poison out. Now, this type of 'tarantulaism' has completely disappeared from the south, but some music and dances have remained. The Tarantula dance evolved from the rites honoring Dionisius and from this further evolved the Pizzica, which you are about to witness." As he spoke these words, my imagination conjured up a peasant woman whirling and screaming in a field after a spider bite and musicians running to her aid, banging on their tambourine and playing the violin while letting her writhe in pain. It almost seemed sexual, as if Dionisius was still casting his spell. I wonder how many survived the poison after the music and dancing were over?

"But the Pizzica is a little different," Mauro continued. "The first records of this dance are from the 1700s; Ferdinand IV, the Bourbon King, was present at a royal ball where the Pizzica was performed..." As he was speaking, the chatting of the patrons died down while the music rose. The chosen man stood on the sidelines while the Pizzica dancer, scarf in hand, began getting a feel for the music, first swaying slowly as we all stared at her. Her eyes were fixed as if, as she began to dance, her mind was in another place and time.

The tambourine and castanets provided the rhythm, while the accordion blended with the guitar and fife, creating a type of music with a gypsy-like quality. The dancer herself began echoing the beat with her castanets; it almost gave the impression that she was in charge of the dance floor and the musicians on the side. "Notice that the music is starting slow," Mauro whispered in my ear. "She is establishing the rhythm, which will eventually accelerate. She will invite the man to dance with her at a certain point. In this Pizzica, you will notice the roles between the man and the woman, but not all Pizzica are dances of courtship. It is widespread to dance the Pizzica at family gatherings, between brother and sister, grandfather and granddaughter, and even between two men."

At this point, the woman invited the man to join her. She tucked her castanets away, took out her long red scarf, and held part of her skirt with one hand. The music began to accelerate just a bit as the man approached. Both had a composed and upright posture as the man, at one point, mirrored the steps of the woman and, at other times, alternated with complementary movements. "Notice," Mauro whispered, "that he tries to look her in the eyes, but she never lets him." I had noticed that the man was trying to pierce her with his look. She, however, either looked down, to the side or above his head. It was as if he were trying to violate her with his eyes, but she would have none of it, strong enough to fend him off.

As the couple turned and swirled, Mauro whispered again, "She is expressing her beauty and femininity through her clothing and her composed dance steps. Notice that sometimes she expresses joy and euphoria with the turns and steps that throw the man off. And notice that her arms are closed, not welcoming the man to any embrace." Just then, the man startled us by leaping and landing loudly on his boots. He had his arms open as if to embrace the woman if she would let him. Suddenly he leaped again, and I looked at the others at our table inquisitively. "The man," Mauro began, "is now expressing his strength and virility; he is taking higher jumps and more rapid movements to show his athleticism and that he is a worthy mate. And look at her reaction," he concluded. The woman continued her dance, sometimes seeming to flirt with him but never letting him get too close and never allowing his eyes to meet hers. She began taking dance steps that seemed like small escapes, sudden stops, and restarts as if she were teasing the man to hunt her. She communicated with her feet and expression as she gazed beyond him.

Suddenly, the music accelerated, and the intensity seemed to grow as the pursuit continued. The crowd became caught up as some began to clap in time with the music, faster and faster. It was as if everything was headed for a climax. What would happen? Would she surrender? Would she push him off? What would she, who controlled the story in this dance, do next? We all wondered as both partners danced faster, he leaped higher, and her feet seemed to blur under her dress. The crowd started to cheer as the dancing and music reached a crescendo. It seemed impossible that two bodies could move so quickly, with such intricate dance moves, leaping and twirling, faster and faster; I had to look away for a moment to regain my focus.

Then, suddenly, the music reached a fever pitch; the woman leaped in the air, the man landed on his knee, and suddenly the music stopped! Everyone was frozen. There was a pause of silence as the dancers panted for breath. Then the crowd, including our table, rose to their feet to clap and cheer this story in music and dance. "Wow," I said out loud. I was speechless.

Suddenly the two dancers were back in the present. He bowed to her, and she smiled at him; he rejoined his family at the table, and she walked next to the musicians. Again, we were in the present, and I realized that we had been transported.

After a few minutes, plates could be heart clanking and glasses clinking as the attention shifted from the dance floor back to our tables. "Do you like?" Mario asked. I had to pause before I could respond. "It was amazing."

The music played lower in the background as we finished our meal and chatted, but there was a sense of awe that had come over all of us that made us speak a little lower and dwell on the world that the Pizzica opened up for us.

Leaving the restaurant, we wandered through the beautiful historical center of Nardo'; the lights were shining on the cathedral, and the central piazza was illuminated. "Culture comes down to us through music, dance but especially through the people," Mauro said. "Yes, but the part that impressed me the most was the way that he looked at her, and she looked beyond him. It's almost like a story that transports you to another time and place," I replied. Mauro nodded. "Yes, that is why the Pizzica is so important to us. It connects us to our past and reminds us of who we are."

Chapter 10
The Towers of Salento

"Are you going to get coffee in Santa Caterina this morning?" Mauro texted. It was 7:30 in the morning; I looked at David, showed him the text, and he nodded. "Yes, we will be there in about an hour," I texted back. "We will meet you there," he responded.

On the Ionian Sea, Santa Caterina is a town for beach lovers. However, in the mornings, we enjoy driving to the cafe in front of the small bay overlooking the turquoise waters. "A perfect way to start the day," I said as we sat down at our outdoor table less than an hour later. We came here often enough that the waiter knew what we wanted before placing our order. "The usual, no?" he asked, and I gave him a thumbs up.

We relaxed and sipped our first coffee while waiting for our Italian friends. A few people were already on the beach, getting set up for their day of sun. There was a scuba rental store nearby, doing brisk business, as patrons and guides walked in and out, loaded with gear. My eye was then drawn back to the beach, to a woman in a thong chatting with her little daughter, pointing to the water. I laughed. "It's funny that we associate a thong with sexuality, and there is this mom wearing one as she spends the day at the beach with her child!" David smiled and nodded. "Maybe our unconscious puritanism leads us to see sex where there is only a body," I continued. David nodded again, sipping. I think his mind was more on his coffee than on the beach.

Our four friends soon arrived, and soon we were all gathered around a small table with more coffees, croissants, and other pastries. Soon we were chatting about the previous evening, our friends in Naples, the people on the beach, the beautiful water, and a myriad of other topics in the space of ten minutes. "What's that?" I broke in, nodding in the direction of the ruins of a tower on the other side of the cove. Our friend Mauro nodded, looking at the building and then at us. "It is worth visiting after breakfast. Do you like it?" he asked. We smiled. He always asked us if we liked everything.

After we had our fill, we drove a short distance, piled out of our cars, walked to the ruins of the tower, and sat on the steps. The cool morning air was perfect as we listened to the waves of the sea lapping below. "Why was this built?" I asked our Italian friends. Mauro turned to me and asked, "Would you like me to tell you the story?" I nodded, glancing at David.

Mauro stood up in front of us and pointed to the opposite shoreline. "Do you remember when we visited Otranto, and we saw those skulls in the cathedral?" All of us nodded in unison. "This story begins there," he said, sitting down on a rock facing us. "I teach this history to my students, so I can fill you in if you want," he continued.

"It was in the 1400s, Constantinople, now known as Istanbul, fell to the Ottoman Turks and became the center of an aggressive empire. Their leader was Sultan Mehmet the Conqueror, and he lived up to his name. His dream was to capture Rome and proclaim himself as the new emperor, uniting the East and West. So he sent over ninety ships and almost 20,000 men to Italy. His fleet aimed towards Brindisi but got blown off course and landed near Otranto. The Ottomans marched towards Otranto, which about 400 soldiers protected; 18,000 Ottomans against 400! The citizens refused to surrender, so the Ottomans attacked the walls, while the people dumped boiling oil, hot water, molten metal, and even furniture on the invaders' heads! The soldiers fought for about two weeks until the Ottomans breached the walls; then the slaughter began."

Mauro took a breath and looked at us to see if we were following along; he then crossed over to a low wall overlooking the beach. "When the invasion was over, all 400 soldiers had been killed; there were only 800 men left alive in the city, who were not fighters. The townspeople of Otranto were weak, starving, and exhausted. Once captured, these 800 men were brought before an Ottoman commander called The Pasha. He gave the captives a choice: choose Islam and live, choose Christianity and die. One of the prisoners stepped forward, turned towards the others, and encouraged them to not fear giving up their lives for their belief. The Pasha became angry, and he ordered the men to be executed. The following day those 800 were marched up the Hill of Minerva, near Otranto. One by one, they were beheaded, and their bodies dumped into a pit.

"After years of battles, eventually, the Ottomans were driven out; the remains of the 800 were then recovered. These are now behind the altar in the cathedral, which you saw." Mauro paused and let the images of his story sink in.

Moving again in front of us, like an Oxford professor, he continued. "These towers result from this and other invasions of this area of Italy. Over and over again, Ottoman aggressors and pirates came to this area to pillage, conquer, rape, and subdue the people. So these towers stem from this era. If you notice," he continued, motioning us to stand up, "that the towers are in a line all up and down the coast. Look. They are spaced so that a signal can be passed from tower to tower, using smoke by day and fire by night. This signal would alert the citizens that ships were sighted. This system greatly increased their defensive capabilities. The locals learned from the siege of Otranto since that city was unprepared for the Ottoman assault. So you can see," he concluded, "that the invasion of Otranto and these towers are connected.

"Let's walk around to see the other side of the tower," Mauro invited us. We followed as he took up the narrative again. "Most of the towers were built in the fifteenth and sixteenth century; there are about sixty standing today, some better preserved than others. Now think about this," he said, touching the wall. "We come to this place as tourists and admire the architecture and atmosphere here, but when they were built, they were places of fear. Imagine two or three soldiers stationed here at night, looking out at sea. Imagine how they felt when they saw the lights from ships out on the water, trying to creep up to the coast for an invasion. They would then uncover the fire to signal the towers down the coast to assemble troops before the ships arrived. The men in these towers knew that they might be outnumbered; they all remembered the massacre at Otranto. They knew that the sign of an unknown ship could mean death. They were thinking these thoughts when they stood in this tower and watched. Imagine that..."

At this point, Matteo, our friend and art historian took over. "Now look at the base of the tower, here," he said, motioning. "The construction of the towers followed certain common guidelines. Here at the bottom was the cistern, which gathered and stored rainwater. Usually, the base was square and, if you look up a level, you can see the remains of the guardhouse. Do you see?" he asked as we squinted and nodded. "At least two soldiers operated each tower. One was cavalry, with his horse below, and another a soldier of some type. They also had a canon, guns, and other weapons. These weapons were used to delay the attackers to allow for the evacuation of the people in the area.

"Do you see these stairs here?" he asked. We nodded since we were now sitting on them again. "These were added later. There were no stairs here. The soldiers lowered a wooden ladder if a friend or ally needed to get in. Then they brought the ladder up so enemies would have difficulty climbing the walls since the soldiers here could shoot at them or dump boiling oil or water on invaders. What a great system!"

"So the towers were armed, fortified with food and water, and the cavalryman could jump on his horse at a moment's notice should he need to carry messages to evacuate those living in the interior areas. The sheer walls of the tower made them hard to climb; this was all an amazing and efficient warning system, and each tower was prepared to fight if the need arose."

Edoardo pushed Matteo aside and gave us some backstory. "The construction of the first defense towers in this area began in the 11th century; it was part of the Norman control of Puglia. This region came under the domination of the Angevin Empire for about two hundred years. The cities were fortified under the reign of Charles of Anjou; he left a record of the first towers built to defend against the invasions of the Saracens. With the invention of gunpowder, these ancient towers became obsolete and were replaced by the towers built in the sixteenth century, which Matteo was explaining..."

Edoardo paused when he heard Matteo, his closest friend, snoring loudly to get him to stop. Matteo then rose, pushed Edoardo aside, and continued. "Now that we have all had a little nap while Edoardo was talking, we can hear about some interesting things..." Though Edoardo started to jeer him, Matteo continued. "You have to imagine the fear. Think of it. In the fifteenth and sixteenth centuries, the people of this entire territory never took their gaze off the horizons. The mast of a ship could mean a massacre. Even with the towers, the raids continued because the forces were often ineffective against emergency attacks. So even farmhouses were fortified to protect the poor farming families. In the late fifteen hundreds, the local rulers organized a more effective military force. For a time, the people felt protected. But armies cost money, and the people had to pay taxes for the upkeep of the soldiers. But with the sea full of pirates and invaders, trade to this region stopped; the military presence was expensive, so the locals could not sustain the military here. To survive, the people abandoned these coastal areas and moved inland, and invaders started to come and go as they pleased. They landed on the shores, took provisions from farms, terrified families, then left. It was terrible! The coastal areas became marshy and full of weeds and mud, with few living there."

Matteo looked around to see if we were listening. "So the invasions continued after the invasion of Otranto, until 1571. Do you remember the painting in the Vatican of the Battle of Lepanto?" David, sitting next to me, nodded. "It is that famous battle that pushed the Turks so far back that they would never be able to dominate the Mediterranean again. So there was a lot of fear, a huge loss of life, and abandoned lands. But also many heroes and those who stood up, not only for their land but also for their beliefs. And these towers embody this history."

We were silent for a while, reflecting on the images of battles, beliefs, and martyrdom. I rested my hand on a stone nearby, thinking of the people in that tower, looking out on the horizon, wondering what the day might bring. We were all lost in thought. Mauro jolted us into the present when he rose and said, "Shall we go?" I rose, patted the stone wall one last time, and we piled into our cars.

What I thought were mere stones and collapsing towers ended up being monuments to courage.

Chapter 11
Lecce: Elegance and Diversity

I have heard that the farther one travels south in Italy, the more homogeneous it becomes. But when I visited Lecce the first time, I was struck by how international the city was. We eventually befriended a man from Egypt, a woman from Ecuador, another from Scotland, and another from Brazil. I wondered what led them to live in Lecce and what their experience has given them thus far.

The interview was free-flowing and lively, giving an insider's and outsider's view of living in Lecce and its diversity.

Tell me about your life.

Letizia: "I am 49 years old, and I was born in Ecuador. I arrived in Italy on January 21 in the year 2000. I remember the day and the hour when I arrived in Florence, where my sister lived. I came because I wanted a better life than I had in Ecuador.

"It took me a while to find work, which I eventually found in Umbria and Tuscany. After living in northern Italy for two years, I came to Lecce, almost by chance, and here I found love. This relationship motivated me to move here in 2004."

Mohsen: "I am a lucky and happy man. I feel satisfied because I am Egyptian and a Sagittarius. I have faith because I believe in a Creator, and in this faith, I find all of my satisfaction.

"I find all of my happiness and satisfaction in this faith. I feel there is a meaning to my life, and I am walking in the right way towards my destiny. I am a married man, I have four kids, and I am so grateful. As a lucky man, I find myself in Lecce, which is the right place for me.

"I love to create and give a message to everyone: to look at the sun and keep the philosophy of the sun. The sun gives to everyone and doesn't ask for anything in return.

"I pray to my Creator to keep me in good health. I am ready to go at any time. These words may seem strange to hear, but I am happy to know that I am going away. One of my happiest moments will be when my body is gone, and my soul is flying to the Creator. Because then I will find what I have been seeking. Until that day, I will keep creating."

Cristina: "I am a journalist, writing about current affairs and arts. I am married to an Italian/Brazilian (he has double citizenship) who is also a journalist and translator. We were tired of living in Sao Paulo, especially with Bolsonaro as president, since he oppresses Brazil. I traveled a lot during my entire life. But I only lived in Sao Paulo. I began to long to change my life.

"The time seemed right. My only daughter, Nina, moved to Barcelona. My parents passed away, and I didn't have other family members in Brazil, so I decided to move to another country. My husband loves Sicily, but we didn't start there. We thought it would be nice to live an almost nomad life, one year in each place. We decided to start this adventure in Lecce."

Margaret: "I grew up in the west of Scotland, but I always had the itch to travel. A friend offered me a job teaching English in a private school in Barletta near Bari in Puglia. I was only there for a few days when I met my future husband Franco, who was there for work but grew up in Lecce. We got married, had children, and eventually moved to Lecce, where my husband's extended family lived. I got a job teaching at a high school in Lecce, where I stayed until I retired in 2013. When my husband passed away in 2012, I focused on the arts and culture, and I even wrote a book about learning English through art."

What made you choose the way of life that you have?

Mohsen: "I feel free. I see many people who do the same thing every day and want to follow someone else's lead. But even when I was a kid, I wanted to pursue something inside me rather than others. For example, when I was very young, I wanted to invent a language just for me. I rebelled against the language that everyone spoke. Something happened in my personality because I wanted to work on myself. I wasn't and am not satisfied to have things, but I feel happy when I can make things.

"Even at a young age, I had the idea that someday I would die. So, what does it mean if I do and have many things, and then I die? So I realized that what I have doesn't matter much; what matters is what I have to give.

"I don't have a job like others, but I still have to support myself and my family. So I was thinking: what about tomorrow if I have no money to buy food? But something inside of me tells me not to worry; tomorrow will take care of itself.

"I sell Egyptian artifacts near one of the historical doors in Lecce; the other day, I was about to head over there during this Christmas season, but it was freezing and rainy, so I decided not to go. I thought I probably wouldn't sell anything. So I decided to stay here, where we are doing this interview, in my shop where nobody ever comes; it is like a desert! But that day I stayed here, and I unexpectedly got a phone call asking if I would make a large carved wooden box, resembling the tomb of a pharaoh, for 1,000 euros! So this is how it works for me; God, the Creator, always takes care of me. For me, yes, for the others, I suppose it works for them too!

"Here I am, 55 years old. I've never been depressed. Yes, I've experienced punishment when I haven't followed my conscience. But when I do follow this way, I am happy. I am satisfied and happy with this way. Maybe I don't have a credit card, but when I need ten euros, somehow I get it! This is a very, very good way for me."

What do you think of Puglia?

Letizia: "I think of Puglia as a beautiful land. The sea, the food, and the people are so kind. I lived in northern Italy, where the people are more closed; I find the people here more open. The sea here is so clean. In Ecuador, the waves are tall, and I am afraid of the sea there; here, I am not scared."

Mohsen: "Puglia is a beautiful place. There are many things and people that help you live a quiet life. The only challenge is that everything is slow. If you want to bring an idea to realization, it takes a long time. Nothing is perfect. But the good thing for me is that it is not crowded, people are calm, and it is always sunny. The food is excellent, people here are very kind and respectful.

"For business, things are slow, but there is a lot of potential in this area. The only thing needed is a leader who loves this land and is not afraid of the north or politics. Politics is far from my thinking, but I will only say that our political leaders in this area could do more to build up this area."

Margaret: "My thoughts on Puglia are rather complex. I have lived all over this region and taught in schools with diverse populations. But I enjoy living here; I have some amazing friends in all places I have lived, even now. The food is exceptional, the landscapes and sea coasts stunning."

What is your experience with other Pugliesi?

Letizia: "I feel at home with the Pugliesi. Only one time, I can recall something negative. A woman living here told me that we immigrants came to steal their husbands! Now I laugh, but then I was offended. But she was the exception."

Mohsen: "They are good people, but most Pugliesi don't seem curious. They talk and support your goals, but there is no action. They are content with what they have; though they have dreams, they have difficulty realizing them. They don't want to risk what they have to create something new.

"For example, I cannot give my word in my culture if I don't know that I can deliver. I make sure I fulfill my promises. But here, your promise may not count as much. They make promises, but there is no fulfillment. They talk a lot and promise much, but they don't deliver; I discovered this cultural difference. But I don't try to change people.

"One quality that I like about the Pugliesi is that they are a quiet people. They are not a disruptive people, and they respect you for your work. In Egypt, the mentality is different. If I were in Egypt and ran a shop and employed people, my employees would be trying to become shop owners and become disruptive. Here that is not the case; the Pugliesi respect my work."

Margaret: "I have three children, and they are more Pugliese than Scottish! The first two were born in Scotland, but they were brought up here and are proud of being Pugliese.

"That said, living in a small town has shown me a more timid, almost archaic side to the people here; they are not always easy to get on with. They say here, 'Leccesi, falsi e cortesi' (People from Lecce: courteous and fake), as with all sayings, enough of a generalization to trigger a host of 'but I know a lot who are not…' and that is true also. It is difficult here to gauge reactions and understand that sometimes their desire to give you the answer you want leads to them not being entirely truthful."

What is your favorite thing or place in Puglia and why?

Letizia: "A place that I love is Porta Selvaggio, which is a nature reserve. I love going there during the Spring and Fall. When I am there, I feel like I am flying to Ecuador. There are beautiful rocks and incredible panoramas. It reminds me of a place in Ecuador where I used to go when I was sad.

"Sometimes I miss Ecuador; my mother is there, and one of my daughters lives there. It makes me emotional when I think of these things. I want to return there next year when my daughter graduates from college."

Mohsen: "I love the sea. The sea here makes me feel at home since I was born near the sea in Egypt. I love feeling the effect of the sun, which is more transparent near the sea. The sea represents contact with other shores, other parts of the world. You can see nature clearer at the sea.

"The sea mirrors this spiritual part. For example, you don't just go fishing when you go fishing. Fishing is a philosophy; you go to think and reflect. So at sea, you have the opportunity to reflect on the project of life (excuse my English).

"Our life is a project beyond work. You need time to reflect on the project of life and one of the best moments to reflect on life is at sea.

"Many of the great philosophers were near the sea and from there derived their inspiration.

"In Puglia, I love the sea, seafood, and the people around the sea.

"Even the people around the sea have different qualities: good and honest people. The sea keeps you drawn towards the spiritual because you are in contact with an unfinished and almost unlimited horizon. A farmer thinks of his land and what he can produce. But the man at the sea has unlimited space in front of his eyes, so he does not count what he has. His gaze focuses on the horizon, and he is more drawn to life in another world. A man at the sea sees life differently than a man chained to the land.

"When they go to eat, seafood is very simple. A piece of fish and bread are all the fisherman needs. But the man in the city needs lots of complex foods to be satisfied. So life is different at the sea.

"When the sun rises and sets, the man at sea has direct contact. This man looks at life differently than the man in the city. So I love the sea and the men living there."

Margaret: "I lived in Foggia for 20 years or more, and when we moved here, I never tired of walking through the narrow streets of Lecce or Otranto, drinking in the visual beauty. I have many different places I never tire of, Otranto, Lecce itself, to name only two."

What is challenging about living here?

Letizia: "The most challenging thing is finding work. When I lived in central Italy with my daughter, I had no job for a while, and it was so difficult. Nobody helps you out. But little by little, I made connections and eventually found work. Now I feel like I am part of the people and culture here."

Mohsen: "To be independent is challenging. Knowing how to keep yourself satisfied and keep yourself in your world can be difficult, and keep yourself quiet and modest. Jealousy can manifest if you stand out and show off your accomplishments or possessions. So to be humble is a critical quality here.

"The man who practices his religion as something that he does only on Sunday and doesn't put it into practice is subject to jealousy. I experienced this. I mind my own business and do my work, but someone lashed out at me in envy. The man who did this is poor on the inside. He didn't listen to his conscience.

"Not just in Puglia, but many have the same jealousy problem; the challenge is to know how to move in the space you have. And to show the courage you possess."

Margaret: "There are many challenging things here, corruption, chaotic traffic, lack of punctuality, laissez-faire attitude, indifference to other people's needs - I could go on. I remember I would make proposals at my school for projects for the students; the administration would agree with me, but then sink my proposals."

How is Lecce different from other parts of Puglia?

Letizia: "The first thing is the climate; it is warm and beautiful here. Other differences I see include the food and the warmth of the people. In places I lived before, you can live in the same building and not know the person's name next to you, especially if you are a foreigner.

"But it is different here. I will give you an example: once I got lost and someone here in Lecce not only gave me directions but came with me to where I needed to go. But when I lived in Milan, this never happened. When I got lost and asked for help, the response was 'Sorry, I am not from here,' even when they lived across the street."

Mohsen: "The mentality of Lecce is more sophisticated than, say, Bari or Foggia. For example, people in Lecce tend to be more respectful, educated, and calm. I am not saying that others living in other areas are not, but these are qualities that I see in Lecce. Looking at Lecce on a map, it is surrounded by the sea, which changes the mentality here. There are also descendants of noble families here, contributing to more wealth but not more industry. In Lecce, you find the man who fishes and eats his fish, satisfied with that. When you travel to other parts, you find more people who become prisoners of their business. This is just my opinion, of course."

Margaret: "Lecce is much more elegant - not only the architecture but also the people. It doesn't have the commercial drive you find in Bari. Even their accent sets them apart from the rest of Puglia. Listen to someone from Bari, Taranto, or Foggia and compare it to the Leccesi, and you'll get it straight away."

Describe the mentality of the Leccesi please.

Letizia: "OK, I am going to say something negative here, but I am not saying it is true for everyone in Lecce. But one trait I have noticed is that people from Lecce are always courteous and false. They can seem kind one minute, and the next, they can stab you in the back. Not everyone is like that, but I have noticed it. At the same time, they are very open-minded people. They are also generous. Most Leccesi go to the beach whenever they can. They love going out to eat and then going for a stroll afterward."

Margaret: "They are an 'Isola Felice' - they enjoy and actively cultivate their differences and distance from other Pugliesi. They are rather 'false,' as I said before - they love to keep up appearances and rarely allow you to participate in their inner feelings. The family is a very close-knit unit - but that is true of all of the south of Italy."

What type of work do you do here?

Letizia: "I've lived in Lecce for 18 years, and I work as a caretaker right now."

Cristina: "I am a journalist and writer."

Margaret: "I am now retired, but I used to teach English. First privately in Barletta, then in state schools."

Mohsen: "I have created and am creating a copy of the tomb of Tutankhamen here in Lecce. This tomb has become a place where visitors come, and students visit on field trips.

"I am drawn to the beliefs of the ancient Egyptians. All the wise words of the ancient philosophers and prophets can be found in the papyrus of the ancient Egyptians. The message for man to live in the right way, from his beginning to his end, comes from Egypt.

"Look at the commandments; nine of the ten commandments came from the 42 rules found in ancient Egyptian theology. These 42 rules are found in the so-called *Book of the Dead*. Look at this hieroglyph; it means 'I was not a loud man,' or this one 'I didn't kill anyone' or 'I didn't terrorize anyone.'

"When you read these words, you find yourself in heaven, in another atmosphere. Just ask, and you can find the answer. When you see this, you can fly. Flying means to balance; if you lose one feather, you lose balance. Flying is a kind of satisfaction. You have to be satisfied with yourself to be able to fly.

"One of the 42 rules says, 'I didn't sleep with tears.' This phrase means that I didn't do anything wrong that would make me cry when I sleep. Your heart must be lighter than the feather.

"You have to love and not judge. All the bad people are victims. You have to think about their lives before you punish them. You could smile, and this may be enough to change them. One joke could remind them that we will die someday. Maybe this is a way of helping yourself and others.

"I love and respect what was believed and lived in ancient Egypt. And I found in myself a miracle to teach, live, and share what I have discovered there.

"In my tomb project, I teach about loving, respecting, and having one's gaze fixed on higher things. To fly, feel happy, and feel satisfied. Through my tomb project, I teach that we will be reborn in another life. To be able to love your destiny and to love being born again. It is essential not to be afraid of dying; these fears have no meaning and can cause us to live a bad life. You have to live well to die well. It seems like a contradiction.

"I found the help of my Creator to create this tomb project. Man needs a key to understand himself. The main goal we have is to know ourselves. If you do not know yourself, you cannot be satisfied. A satisfied man can explain who he is.

"It is the voice of the Creator inside of you: the conscience. You feel this energy when you study yourself; when you are there, the one who made you is there. When you are not there, there is nothing. The man who lives from nothing, how can he become satisfied? I believe this, which is why I found great success in creating this tomb. I love the visitors who come, the school children, to share my stories about what I learned from the ancient Egyptians.

"Something happened to me to make me very satisfied and very happy; it all comes from him, from the Creator. All the tomb comes from me, my hands, and my ideas. It was not given to me. Once I am gone, I feel that there will be a place in Lecce where something about ancient Egypt will be shared.

"This tomb is a philosophy; there are no guards here, nobody comes to steal. The Creator protects it. This tomb will keep telling these stories because it flows from the Creator. The words that have been spoken for over 10,000 years are still being shared today, here, in Lecce."

How long will you live here?

Cristina: "I think we will live in Lecce for about one year. When my husband and I decided to come to Italy, our idea was to live one year in each region. We stayed two years in Sicily thanks to the pandemic."

Margaret: "I am going to die here. I am going to celebrate my 50 years in Italy in September. Although I have two of my children near Cambridge, brothers and sisters, nephews, and nieces all over Great Britain, I am 'stuck' here. I have a house which I think would be difficult to sell, a daughter who lives in San Cesario, but, more importantly, a lack of enthusiasm to move anywhere - maybe just too lazy?"

What gives you joy about living here in Puglia?

Mohsen: "My happiness has to come from within, from the way that I live my life. Without this happiness, I am a prisoner. In Lecce, I find it easy to build and live in my world. For example, life here is quiet; you can follow life's rhythm without much effort. I can walk from my home to my Egyptian museum, and there are many things I can do with my family and others. I can run to the sea whenever I want; I jog along a green path every day. People are respectful; some say hello, some not, but they are all kind. Just like all Italians, they have bad language and curse words, but the people in Lecce are quiet and do not swear in public. They want to present themselves as good people and want to have a good image, and this is very important. Even people who are not so good are concerned about their image, and so, in public, they take care of what they do and say."

Margaret: "Joy is a big word! There are some days when the weather is good, not too hot, nor cold, so a walk along the seafront in San Foca is smile-provoking."

Cristina: "Living near nature — stunning beaches."

If you could change something about your life, what would it be?

Letizia: "I would change nothing. I have no regrets, and I embrace all of my life."

Margaret: "I honestly have no idea - or maybe too many! I never wanted to be a teacher, but I was a good one. I don't know if I would have come to Italy - knowing what I do now - but then I wouldn't have met my husband and had three amazing children. I have no regrets."

What is the happiest experience you have had here?

Letizia: "The first thing that comes to mind, I cannot say! The second thing is the sea: the sea gives me life. It gives me joy. It feels like freedom and happiness. If I am nervous, water always relaxes me."

Cristina: "Going along with my dog Zara to Santa Maria di Leuca on my birthday and getting a piece of cake from the waiter in a cafe comes to mind. Swimming in September at so many different beaches, or a surprise pizza with friends... having a great lunch with my daughter who lived in Barcelona and came to visit. These are joyful moments."

Margaret: "Many, many happy things have happened to me here. I found a marvelous man, had three fantastic children; on a less lofty note, I learned to speak Italian like a native, cultivated some great friendships and lots of other little things that, put together, make a good life."

Can you tell us about a funny thing that happened to you here?

Letizia: "I remember that we were at a festival and there were traditional dances which I didn't know. I love to dance, so I got up and danced. Then my daughter, who was very young at the time, danced better than I did. My friends came up to me and whispered, 'Sit down, Letizia! Your daughter dances better than you!' I laughed, then I sat down.

"The one thing I want to add is that life is full of possibilities. I could have remained in Ecuador or returned there with my earnings, but instead, I stayed here. I found love and created a new life here, which makes me very happy."

Cristina: "I went to the supermarket and bought some chicken. The lady who worked as the butcher asked me where I was from. I said 'Brazil,' we then started to talk, etc. I told her I was looking for an apartment to rent, and she said: 'Wait!' Then she called a guy and said: 'Yes, she is Brazilian, my personal friend, she is special, show her your house, treat her well,' (I talked to her for 3 minutes and I didn't know her name). The way she spoke to the guy on the phone and managed the situation was hilarious. She seemed like a mobster. In the end, I didn't even meet her friend."

Margaret: "We were invited to dinner; all four of us arrived with a big box of chocolates in hand. We rang the bell; the husband opened the door with such a look of surprise that we realized he had forgotten or never really intended the invitation seriously. The wife was at the top of the stairs, calling out, 'Who is it? Who IS it?' 'Friends come to dinner,' he replied - her facial expression was comical. 'Never mind,' we say, 'obviously, there's been a mix-up.' 'Noooo, no worries, we'll just add a cup of water to the soup.' 'WHAT' screams the wife' SOUP? SOUP? I haven't made any soup. The original 'allunghiamo il brodo' is a way of saying we'll manage with what we have."

After this interview, it became clear that the people fill the contours of a place; the citizens of Lecce, whether born or immigrated, seem to share the quality of love for their land, their sea, and the peaceful life that this place affords. Seeking adventure, love, a better life, and the sea are common threads that run through the lives of these residents of Lecce. Whether from Egypt or Scotland, Brazil or Ecuador, each left a life behind and began anew in a city known for its baroque elegance and its diverse population.

Chapter 12
Trani: Sex, a Cathedral, and a Homeless Man

The first time I heard about Trani was when we were in the car heading there. We were ready for an adventure with a carload of Italians and two Californians. "Have you heard of Trani before?" our friend Giulio asked. His eyes were on us rather than on the road while he waited for our response. "No!" I said quickly, so he could focus on driving. "There is a beautiful Cathedral there, which I think you will like. But there are also some interesting stories about its past. It has to do with sex. Do you want me to tell you?" His eyes were off the road again as he waited for our response. "Yes!" we both said in unison, both out of interest and a sense of self-preservation.

"Trani,'" Giulio began, "is of Greek origin. It refers to Diomedes, the Greek hero who fought at Troy. Have you heard of him?" I gave a half-hearted nod; yes, something about Troy, yes, OK. Giulio continued: "The name indicates the Greek influence in Trani, and there are indications that there was a Greek community there when the town was founded. The dates are uncertain, but there has certainly been a settlement here for a thousand years and perhaps much longer." My mind was starting to wander. When are we going to get to the sex part? "The Greeks had much more blurred lines between heterosexuality and homosexuality..." My ears perked up. "It became known, until very recently, that the fishermen of Trani were always available for sex with other men, even though they had wives, children, and families. Men came to Trani to encounter these fishermen, and their fame for blurring sexual lines became well known in certain circles. David nodded. "In gay circles?" I laughed, but Giulio continued. "There were not always 'gay circles' and 'straight circles,' but the word was passed around that in Trani you could find what you wanted."

There was a pause in the car as each of us created images of what Giulio was describing. Then the inevitable question came from me: "So is this still happening today?" David piped in: "Can we go see the fishermen? To see with our own eyes!" Giulio chuckled. We all stared at him. Our curiosity was genuine, and here he was laughing! "Let's pick up the speed and get to the fishing dock!" I thought to myself. "This was in the past. The culture has changed so much that being gay has become mainstream, no longer a secret thing between visitors and fishers. I am sorry to tell you 'no,' as far as I know, there is no longer this reputation of meeting the fishermen in Trani for sex. In fact, with the commercialization of fishing, few fishermen are left there. So, today, most people come to Trani to see the beautiful cathedral and walk through the historical center. That is what we will do." We all faded back into our seats, a bit disappointed as the sordid lives of fishermen were fading from our imaginations.

We were silent during the last kilometers of our drive. Giulio found a parking spot outside the historical area; we piled out and followed his lead. Turning a corner, we were awestruck. Before us was the cathedral, a vast Romanesque building erected right on the water! The sea and the cathedral seemed to form an incredible unity of beauty that stopped us in our tracks. "Do you like it?" Giulio asked. Our other Italian companion, Marco, answered for us as we were silent. "From the expression on their faces and their mouths hanging open, I think they like it." After a pause, Giulio encouraged us to approach the church. "It gets better on the inside. Keep in mind that this church has been standing for almost a thousand years. It sits on the foundations of another church built on this spot in the fourth or fifth century. I want you to see how the interior of the church reflects the history of this place." We strolled behind him, always looking up at this impressive structure. "Have they been struck dumb?" Giulio asked Marco. Marco nodded.

As we approached the church, Giulio started his narration in the background. I found myself half-listening as he described the origins of the white limestone molded into a beautiful example of Romanesque architecture. We stopped at the front doors. "Just the doors date from the 1100s, but these are copies. The originals are inside. But look at the figures at the doors, which carry your eye from figures found on earth, like plants and animals, to spiritual images. The doors are an invitation to lift your spirit before entering."

"Who is the church dedicated to?" I asked. "St. Nicholas the Pilgrim. He was from Greece. Have you heard of him?" The blank expressions on our faces answered his question. "Well, let's imagine who he was..." he began.

We found some steps outside the church, where we sat as Giulio began the tale. His words turned into images; I imagined I could hear the mother of this man, Nicholas, recount the history.

"I am ashamed to reveal the details of this story and the part I played, but healing comes from admitting one's fault, and forgiveness begins from oneself. So I will tell you the truth. We were poor; my husband and I were farmers; we had a few sheep, and we raised our two sons in Steiri, Greece. The year Nicholas was born was the year of our Lord, 1075. He was eight when he took over as shepherd of our few sheep, and he took them out every day at dawn and came back at dusk. Perhaps this was my first mistake: to leave our young son alone so much. It was after some months in the pastures that, one day, Nicholas returned home changed. He kept calling out in a loud voice, 'Kyrie Eleison!' which, in your language, means 'Lord have mercy!' Now, this isn't strange in itself, but he would repeat it over and over and over again. He was up all that night, calling out this phrase. My other son here," she said, motioning to Nicholas' brother Georgios sitting next to her, "was too young to remember. But I thought Nicholas to be feverish and dismissed it. The next morning he left for the sheep; it was mid-morning that a neighbor knocked at my door and told me that our sheep had run off across the hills, afraid of Nicholas, who continued to call out 'Kyrie Eleison!' I went out to find him and found the boy chasing the sheep around the grasslands, calling out all the while, 'Kyrie Eleison!' 'Nicholas!' I called out. 'Stop that shouting! The sheep will never return! You are scaring them!' But he kept calling out, 'Kyrie Eleison!' I didn't know what to think, but at that point, I was angry. 'Go home to your father,' I ordered him as I chased down the sheep."

The woman looked down as if she could see the images she described. She sighed before she continued. "Now, my husband was not well. We managed the best we could. Though his father needed longer rest periods than most people, Nicholas continued to call out 'Kyrie Eleison!' during the whole day and often at night. Weeks passed, then months, and as my husband's health deteriorated, my capacity to adapt to Nicholas' behavior withered. I even beat the boy, thinking I could force him to stop. But he continued disturbing the family and the neighbors. He became known as the village fool. But now I believe that Nicholas could not change..."

At this, Georgios joined the conversation. "He could not change because his problem was here," he said, pointing to his head.

"Whether that is true or not," his mother responded, "he was my son and your brother."

She continued: "I know it was wrong of me, and I regret it, but when he was twelve years old, I told Nicholas to leave. I told him that there is no room for him or his behavior under this roof and that he must be gone by the morning.

"To my surprise, when I awoke in the morning, Nicholas was gone. I can't describe the peace in that house! Quiet and restful for the first time in years. But it was in those quiet days that my husband died."

"Mother!" Georgios intervened. "Tell them about the cave! Can I tell this part?" The woman nodded. "Stories started to circulate that Nicholas lived nearby in a cave, surviving on grass and berries. Rumors started about him being mistreated by my mother. People said he was a poor sickly fool abandoned by his family. I went to ask the priest in our village what we should do. The man looked at me and asked if we hadn't already done enough! He made me feel bad. Then I asked him if he knew how my brother was. He did have some news. He told me that Nicholas had befriended a monk known to our priest and that this monk visited Nicholas in the cave and taught him about God and faith and the monastic life. He said that Nicholas continues to call out 'Kyrie Eleison!' but this didn't bother him. The monk told him that the boy had a good heart and had suffered much for one so young. So I returned to my mother, weeping, and told her the story."

"I am an ignorant woman," his mother began. "When I heard this news, my heart did not soften. I became convinced that Nicholas was under the influence of the evil one. I heard examples in the village of how demons can possess people and make them call out. So we set out to find him and, when we spotted him at the entrance of the cave, he stood there looking at us. He looked me in the eyes; I can still see his gaze. Then the boy looked away. He knew what I was up to; he saw no empathy in my eyes. I brought two men with me; we took the boy from the cave and brought him to the monastery of St. Luke in our region. There I told the monks, 'The boy is possessed. Please keep him until you cast out the demons.' And do you know what poor Nicholas said? He just looked up and said, 'Kyrie Eleison!' The two men who helped me laughed; the prior of the monastery smiled, and we left Nicholas there, twelve years old, by himself. We didn't even say goodbye.

"The boy lasted a few months at the monastery; we are now friends with one of the monks, who told us that the monks thought they could force him out of this stupor as he shouted 'Kyrie Eleison!' The boy was beaten, locked in a tower, and even thrown into the sea. All of this failed, and the monks concluded that the boy was not possessed but was a fool. Some of those so-called 'holy men' laughed at him while others just gossiped about the child. But this monk, a holy man, told me that our son was a fool for God and that he was beloved. Eventually, the abusive monks at the monastery of St. Luke even realized this, and they offered him to stay." The woman had regained her composure and was now telling the story with some enthusiasm. "But the boy shook his head, said one last 'Kyrie Eleison!' and walked out. He was home again the next day."

Her son took over the narrative again. "When he returned, Nicholas was good for nothing. He was so loud that the neighbors complained about his 'Kyrie Eleison!' Nicholas and I started to go up into the hills every day to get him away from the house. I would throw rocks and play and shout to hear my echo, but Nicholas would carve crosses all day and plant them in trees, on hilltops, along roads, everywhere! Sometimes I thought it was funny, but I remembered that he was my brother.

"One day, I fell asleep, with Nicholas next to me. I don't know how I slept, with him always calling out 'Kyrie Eleison!', but I did. When I awoke, somehow we were on the highest peak of the surrounding hills; I don't remember walking there. Perhaps Nicholas carried me. However it happened, when I awoke, Nicholas said he had a dream, and in the dream, some divine creature told him that if we stayed here for three days, the destinies of our lives would be revealed. At this, I grew cross and angrily told him, 'So not only do you want to be a hermit, but you want to drag me with you? What about our poor mother? You would abandon her?' Nicholas responded, 'God will provide for her.' I was furious at this; I turned and left Nicholas on that spot." The boy paused, wiped his eyes, and concluded: "That was the last time I ever saw him."

"We also heard the story about the monk Maximus, who was also at the monastery of St. Luke," Nicholas' mother added. "He found him in the mountains, planting crosses and calling out 'Kyrie Eleison!' The monk passed by on a horse, but Nicholas stepped in front of him, forcing him to stop. Then my boy said to this monk, who was not a good man, 'Why do you mistreat your workers and oppress those under you?' Maximus then got down from his horse and beat Nicholas with a stick while the boy called out, 'Kyrie Eleison!' When he finished with him, this monk rode off. The stories passed around this area claim that, for the rest of his life, Maximus would lie awake every night because he could not escape the sound of 'Kyrie Eleison!' in his head.

"There were other stories about how my son suffered, some true, others false. There was one about a woman who accused him of seducing her, a lie. But there is the true story of how the abbot of St. Luke humiliated Nicholas by refusing to give him communion and having him cast out of the cathedral on the feast of St. Cosmas and Damien. The bystanders said that the boy wept for many hours outside the church. At this time, he decided he would leave Greece to travel to Rome. Perhaps there, he probably thought, he could find acceptance."

The boy took up the narrative again. "His problems began on the ship from Greece. My brother kept shouting 'Kyrie Eleison!'; the men on deck became scared. They just wanted him to be quiet, but Nicholas couldn't help himself. When the captain ordered him beaten, he kept calling out, 'Kyrie Eleison!' But then a great storm fell upon the ship; the captain thought they wouldn't survive. 'Pray to God if you have his ear,' he pleaded with Nicholas. So, of course, my brother called out, over and over again, 'Kyrie Eleison!' When the storm calmed, finally, Nicholas was treated with respect.

"I have a friend who lives in Otranto, and he told me some of the stories surrounding my brother. Nicholas carried all the problems with him from Greece to Italy. He arrived in Otranto and kept shouting 'Kyrie Eleison!' Theodore, the bishop of that place, soon became his enemy and thought my brother a fool. But something else began to happen; people started to come to Nicholas to ask them to pray for this, to pray for that. 'Pray that my daughter is cured,' or 'I am barren; pray that I might have children', or 'I have lost my income; pray that I might find work.' Many of these prayers were answered, so the reputation began to grow that Nicholas was not crazy. He was a friend of God.

"Now, don't get me wrong. My brother wasn't a raving idiot. The stories prove this. In Otranto, for example, during a religious procession, he stopped and greeted a Jewish woman, embraced her, and said that he was grateful that they shared the same father in heaven. For this gesture, Nicholas was persecuted. He was always open to others, accepting, and nonjudgmental. He met a blind man on the road on another occasion, always in Otranto. Feeling compassion, Nicholas knelt next to him and wept. The man, whose name I do not know, told my brother that he had killed a man in his youth for money and that he neither deserved forgiveness nor his sight. It is said that Nicholas gave him both.

"He began to travel at this point, always shouting out 'Kyrie Eleison!', which always got him into trouble. Eventually, Nicholas ended up at Taranto, where his 'Kyrie Eleison!' reached the ears of Bishop Albert. Regarding my brother as a trouble maker, he had Nicholas whipped so severely that the ground around him was red with his blood."

His mother was weeping now, but she insisted on stepping in and finishing this account. "In Trani, there was a small church in honor of the Virgin. My son left Taranto for Trani, bleeding and weak. Everywhere he went, he encountered suffering and persecution. He intended to go to Rome but could only make it to Trani. He went to that church and collapsed on the steps. The priest saw him and ran out to see what the matter was. This priest realized that Nicholas was dying and heard my son's last words. My son forgave us all.

"They tell me that they are building a church on that spot, above the church of the Virgin, in honor of Nicholas. I am so grateful. He suffered much in this life and never found a place to belong. But now the people of Trani love him; he is 'their' saint."

His brother concluded the story with this reflection. "What I realized is that what matters, in the end, is not whether someone is normal or crazy, intelligent or stupid, educated or not. What matters is the heart, what someone loves. Nicholas taught me this. He was God's fool, the one who would show all of us what is important and what is folly. In truth, he was the wisest of all of us..."

"And that is the story of Nicholas," Giulio concluded as I came out of my trance. This is truly a special place; such a glorious church in honor of a homeless man, a fool for God.

We were silent as we approached the enormous front doors. "From sex-crazed fishermen to the mad homeless guy who finally found acceptance! This place is full of wonders!" David blurted out. Giulio turned to us and whispered, "You haven't seen anything yet." Then we crossed the threshold and entered the darkened church.

Conclusion

Two Californians came to Puglia for friendship and found a people with open arms, a rich history influenced by Greece and Rome, and a land embedded not only with olives but with stones that recount stories of courage, industry, faith, and loyalty.

"Puglia is what dreams are made of," a friend said to me during that first trip. I scratched my head, looked at him to see if he was joking, and then kept driving. "That doesn't make any sense," I thought to myself as endless olive trees flew by the window. It takes time for a relationship to grow, and Puglia, over time, began to reveal her secrets.

In Bari, we encountered St. Nicholas and the story that led to his being laid to rest in this city. His tomb became a symbol of different faiths working together for peace. As we entered the area of Alberobello, we understood the value of friendship and met some expats who dared to give up everything to start a new life. Why did they leave? Why did they come to Puglia? What did they find? These questions opened up new horizons as we listened to their stories.

The difference in mentalities between California and Pugliesi bubbled to the surface as we spent an evening at a farmhouse, a masseria, and then journeyed to participate in a living Nativity scene for Christmas. Sometimes irritating and other times humorous, these encounters of mentalities enriched and challenged us to judge less and enlarge our cultural benchmarks.

When we finally went to Otranto, we were not only spellbound by the 1,000-year-old design on the Cathedral floor but wondered how such an open mentality towards the world could emerge from a Greek monastery near the coast of Italy a thousand years ago. Perhaps this history helps to understand the mindset in Puglia today, which tends to be more open than the extreme north.

Mesmerized by the storytelling in the dances in Nardo', we realized that one particular dance is not merely moving one's limbs to rhythm, but that the histories are handed down not only through written and oral tradition but also through the magic of movement.

Having a coffee at Santa Caterina, we discovered the towers of Salento, representative of fear, defense, and courage. We could stand in that place where soldiers guarded this land and fought off invaders.

Lecce is the land of elegant architecture and a more diverse population than one would expect. One evening we met Mohsen, an Egyptian living in Lecce who sold artifacts at one of the main entrance gates to the city. We met others from Brazil and Ecuador, and other countries. From these friendships, we discovered that Lecce is home to entirely diverse mentalities, backgrounds, and religious beliefs that thrive together without conflict, each with their own story that led them to this place.

The tales in this work conclude with Trani, one of the most beautiful places in Puglia. A homeless man, perhaps with Tourette Syndrome[1], became a model for others because of how he loved.

It is challenging to define Puglia in one or many words because it means many things to different people. Perhaps the stories here will help show that a tree is not just a tree, a cathedral by the sea is not just a building, and a foreigner is not just another resident. Each has its story, which gives it life, just like the floor of the Cathedral in Otranto.

---

1 Tourette Syndrome (TS) is a condition of the nervous system which causes people to have "tics". There are two types of tics—motor and vocal. Vocal tics are sounds that a person makes with his or her voice. Examples of vocal tics include humming, clearing the throat, or yelling out a word or phrase.